A GUIDE TO
PERSONNEL MANAGEMENT

A GUIDE TO PERSONNEL MANAGEMENT

Mary Green Miner

Consulting Editor and Director, BNA Surveys
The Bureau of National Affairs, Inc.

John B. Miner

Research Professor of Management
Georgia State University

The Bureau of National Affairs, Inc., Washington, D.C.

Printed in the United States of America
Library of Congress Catalog Card Number: 73-77272
International Standard Book Number: 0-87179-185-4 (hardcover)
0-87179-186-2 (paper)

PREFACE

Over the past few years several of our friends and colleagues have suggested we create a volume such as this, combining the first author's knowledge of personnel practice from her work as a BNA editor and director of BNA surveys and the second author's expertise in personnel theory, research, and practice from his role as an industrial psychologist, consultant, researcher, and college professor. The book is designed to provide an overview of what personnel management is, how it has developed to this point in time, what is known from survey and other research that might aid those charged with personnel decision-making, and what the prospects are for the field within the larger framework of general management. Our intended audience includes newcomers to personnel positions, plant personnel managers and other personnel practitioners who would like a brief updating in the field, specialists in human resources who desire a broader picture of what personnel management is in all its many ramifications, and managers in marketing, production, or other departments who would like to obtain a rapid overview of the personnel function in the organization as a whole and within their own departments.

The presentation is deliberately brief. This is not a "how-to-do-it" book, but rather a "what-to-keep-in-mind" commentary to be used in making decisions with regard to human-resource policies and practices. For those who want to explore topics in depth, we have included a list of selected references at the end of the book; for more detail on the results of research studies mentioned throughout the book, the reader is referred to the authors' PERSONNEL AND INDUSTRIAL RELATIONS: A MANAGERIAL APPROACH, Second Edition (Macmillan, 1973); for numerous examples of current company policies and practices, the reader should check BNA's looseleaf service, PERSONNEL MANAGEMENT.

As is inevitable in this type of endeavor, we are indebted to many individuals for their contribution to the end result. It is not possible to name them all; however, we would like to thank in particular the many personnel executives, several of them members of BNA's *Personnel Policies Forum*, who shared their time and their ideas with us. For deciphering and typing the original manuscript we are grateful to the secretarial staffs at the University of South Florida and the University of Maryland. We also would like to express our appreciation to our associates who encouraged this effort to begin with and to John, Cynthia, and Frances Miner and Jill and David Thompson, our children, for their interest in our work and their willingness to share their vacations and holidays with our endeavors.

M.G.M.
J.B.M.

February 1973

TABLE OF CONTENTS

PART III—The Prospects for Personnel Management

PART IV—Source Material

PART I
Personnel in Perspective

CHAPTER 1

Defining Personnel Management

People are the universal resource that organizations must manage. Large or small, public or private, business or nonbusiness, organizations by definition involve human resources. In business firms, the management of human resources is combined with the management of material and monetary resources to achieve the organization's goals; but in some types of organizations, in such fields as government and education, there is little control over the monetary resources available. In these situations, the management of human resources, including personnel management, becomes the most important organizational task.

There is another sense in which personnel management is a universal management activity. According to a well-known adage, "management *is* personnel administration." * In other words, all managers from first-level supervisors to company president or even chairman of the board are engaged in personnel administration in the sense that they are responsible for organizing, directing, motivating, coordinating, and controlling the people under them in the organizational hierarchy. It is this aspect of human resource management, in fact, that creates many of the difficulties that plague personnel people in their work. As we shall note in more detail later, conflicts between line managers exercising staffing and other functions and the personnel expert maintaining standards and control can seriously hamper getting the job done.

Our concern in this book is not with the personnel or human resource responsibilities of managers in general but with the person-

*This observation often has been credited to Lawrence A. Appley, who was president of the American Management Association (AMA) for many years. In the March-April 1969 issue of *Personnel*, however, Appley says that this remark came from the keynote address at an AMA personnel conference in 1937 by Thomas G. Spates, vice-president for personnel of General Foods Corporation.

nel practitioner—the person who in one capacity or another has a hand in formulating personnel policies and in setting up procedures for putting the policies into practice. Among other things, he, or she, may be an assistant to the president of a small concern with responsibilities for purchasing and office management as well as for personnel, a specialist in wage and salary systems for a multiplant corporation with responsibility for administering programs in dozens of operations throughout the country, a plant personnel manager handling all aspects of personnel in one location, or a vice-president charged with responsibility for planning the personnel policies that will affect thousands of employees.

WHAT IS PERSONNEL MANAGEMENT ?

In the broadest sense, personnel management is the process of managing people in all aspects of the employer-employee relationship. While the process itself is universal, the concept of personnel management within specific organizations is far from universal; even the terminology differs widely from one organization to another. Thus, one may find an Employee Relations Department in one company, a Personnel Department in another, Industrial Relations in a third, Manpower Administration in a fourth, Human Relations in a fifth—all performing essentially the same tasks.

Whatever the terminology, the personnel or employee relations function may be defined more precisely in two ways—in terms of the goals it is expected to achieve within an organization and in terms of the work or activities undertaken to realize these goals.

The Goals of Personnel Management

One of the earliest definitions of personnel management in terms of its goals comes from the first textbook published in this country in the field—*Personnel Administration*, by Ordway Tead and Henry C. Metcalf, published in 1920. The authors defined the personnel job as ". . . the direction and coordination of the human relations of any organization with a view to getting the maximum necessary production with a minimum of effort and friction with proper regard for the genuine well-being of the workers."

At the time Tead and Metcalf were writing, personnel was concerned almost entirely with the rank-and-file work force, many of whose number were immigrants and not well educated; the task goal of maximum productivity was paramount. During the period following World War II, another goal emerged as a major concern. This is the goal of maintaining the organization as an entity in the face of pressures and changes both from within and outside the organization itself. This goal often is called *organizational maintenance*, or simply the maintenance goal in contrast to the productivity goal. Organizational maintenance is served by programs such as job enlargement and job enrichment aimed at increasing the level of job satisfaction of today's changing, better-educated group of employees. Employee communication programs are another example of efforts to contribute to the achievement of this goal.

Neither of the two goals—productivity or maintenance—is the exclusive province of personnel management. They are the goals of all areas of management. The personnel department, however, is more likely to be called upon to come up with policies and programs to achieve maintenance goals than to find ways to increase productivity directly. A third goal for management is appearing on the horizon—the goal of social responsibility. This too is a goal that is likely to fall in personnel's bailiwick. We have seen examples in programs such as those for hiring and training the culturally disadvantaged. Initially, at least, these programs do not contribute to achieving the task goal, and they often have resulted in negative effects on organizational maintenance because of conflict with regular employees or supervisors. The only goal served by such programs at this initial point in time is that of social responsibility. Increasingly, management of all types of organizations, but particularly large business organizations, is being called upon to undertake community projects of a social welfare nature. Often it is the personnel department that is given the challenge of finding ways to answer these demands.

These, then, are the major, long-run goals of management—productivity, maintenance, and perhaps social responsibility. All organizations, no matter how large or how long they have been in existence, strive to achieve their productivity or task goals; if these goals are not realized, the organization has no reason to exist. Most organizations also are concerned with maintaining themselves as ongoing enterprises. Some organizations, usually the larger and financially successful ones, are motivated by social responsibility as well. In the long run, however, it may be that the goal of social responsibility will be subsumed as part of the goal of organizational maintenance on the theory that in order to survive, any organization has to be responsive to pressures from its environment.

All these goals are achieved within organizations by setting up short-term objectives and developing programs for realizing them. This is done through the work or activities of the personnel department in cooperation with managers throughout the organization.

The Work of Personnel

While the overall goals of personnel management may be similar across organizations, the short-term goals differ considerably. In one survey more than 200 personnel executives were asked what they considered the primary purpose or objective of their personnel program. The replies were so diverse that the researchers did not even attempt to classify them. In some cases they were quite specific—"to set up and to administer an hourly and salary wage program to keep employees in such a frame of mind that they do not vote a union in"—and in others quite broad—"to convince our employees through actions that our company has their interests at heart."

Just as the short-term goals differ from one organization to another, so also do the specific programs and activities to achieve them. As many as 40 or 50 separate functions may be involved in the work of any one personnel department. In general, however, all the activities that are the responsibility of personnel in most organizations fall into one of the following categories:

Planning—formulating general personnel policies, manpower planning, job analysis, organization planning.

Selection and Assignment—recruiting, interviewing, testing, selection, and placement of new employees; promotion, transfer, and separation of present employees.

Performance Appraisal—employee merit-rating, other measures of productivity and job satisfaction, management appraisal.

Training and Development—orientation, on-the-job training, supervisory training, management development, organization development, educational and scholarship programs.

Wage and Salary Administration—nonmanagement and management pay policies, wage surveys, job evaluation, incentive and bonus plans, executive compensation.

Employee Benefits—vacations, holidays, leaves, insurance, retirement benefits, savings and stock plans.

Employee Services—counseling, recreation and social activities, legal and financial aid, help with housing and moving, parking and feeding facilities.

Employee Relations—discipline, grievance-handling, service and performance awards.

Communications—employee publications, attitude surveys, suggestion systems, community relations.

Work Environment—safety programs, health and medical services, physical working conditions, plant security.

Union Relations—dealing with organizing efforts, collective bargaining, arbitration.

Reports and Recordkeeping—setting up a personnel information system, compiling facts and figures both for internal use and for compliance with government regulations.

The specific activities listed in each category are not intended to be all-inclusive, although they are the ones most frequently associated with the personnel department. Which of these activities will be included in the work of a particular personnel department depends on such variables as company size; whether it is located in an urban area; make-up of the employee group in terms of characteristics like age, sex, education, or skill level; type of industry; extent of unionization; and the value system of top management.

Outside factors also have an impact on personnel activities. In times of full employment and labor shortages, companies may expand their usual training efforts, or undertake new programs, to ensure a supply of employees with the necessary skills. As noted earlier, such programs may be undertaken even in times of high unemployment under pressure from government or social agencies to provide opportunity for the disadvantaged. Thus, both economic and social forces may be reflected in the work of today's personnel department.

A Systems Concept of Personnel

Another way of looking at the personnel function is through a systems concept, which shows how the various activities listed above relate to one another. In this systems concept, the input is people, with their various skills, experience, aptitudes, attitudes, and other characteristics. The output is employee performance, which leads to the achievement of organizational goals. Mediators, or the factors that may affect employee performance, are such things as pay, training, working conditions, and supervisory behavior. This concept may be illustrated as follows:

Input ⟶ Mediators ⟶ Output ⟶
People   Pay   Employee
              Training   Performance
              Working Conditions
              Supervisory Behavior

Contributes to Achievement of Organizational Goals

The activities of the personnel department are involved with the input, mediating, and output *processes*, as illustrated below:

Input Processes	Mediating Processes	Output Processes
Recruiting	Training and development	Management appraisal
Interviewing	Wage and salary programs	Merit-rating
Testing	Benefits and services	Productivity measures
Selection	Discipline, grievances	
Placement	Communications	
Promotion	Safety and health	
Transfer	Manpower and organization planning	
	Job analysis	
	Union relations	

The input processes include all the programs and techniques associated with the hiring of new employees and their placement in specific jobs within the organization. Similarly, the promotion or transfer to new jobs of employees already on the company payroll is an input process with respect to those jobs and the work groups affected. Whether the concern is with new hires or present employees, the aim of the input process is to achieve as ideal a match as possible between the requirements of a particular job and the person selected to fill it.

The mediating processes can be viewed as having several objectives. Some of them are designed to improve the input, such as training programs to provide employees with skills they did not have at the time they were hired, or incentive pay programs to motivate them to higher performance. Some mediating processes are input-sustaining; the purpose of most industrial medical and safety programs is to make sure employee performance does not suffer by reason of illness or accident. Other mediating processes are in the nature of control procedures, such as discipline and counseling, which are called into action when employee performance deteriorates. Their purpose is to try to restore the human input to its previous level, or at least to some acceptable level of performance.

Mediating processes also can be related to the different types of organizational goals. Most of the programs mentioned in the preceding paragraph are oriented to achieving higher productivity and thus relate to task goals. Mediating processes aimed at reducing conflict or improving the work environment, and thus contributing to organizational maintenance, include such activities as union relations, communications, and employee services.

The output processes encompass the procedures used to measure the actual performance of employees and managers in relation to expected performance. These processes should answer the question of how well employee job performance is contributing to the achievement of organizational goals. The output processes also provide information that may indicate the need for adjustments in the input or the mediating processes, on either an individual or a group basis. A consistently low level of production in a particular work group may suggest that the supervisor could use some additional training in how to motivate his employees, that the employees themselves may need more training in how to perform certain tasks, or that the jobs to be done in that group require entirely different abilities from those possessed by the present employees. The determination of the correct solution to such problems is usually a matter of personnel research, which ideally is carried on with respect to all the programs making up the personnel function.

One advantage of the systems view of personnel is that it gives a clear indication of the personnel activities that should be emphasized with respect to various employee groups within an organization. For professional, technical, and managerial personnel, for example, the input processes are most critical—the employer needs to find people who already have the education and training necessary to perform jobs at this level. For entry-level factory jobs, on the other hand, the best approach may be to emphasize the mediating processes by hiring anyone available and providing on-the-job training. The costs of such training could well be less than the costs of an extensive testing and interviewing program to achieve the same result.

PERSONNEL IN THE ORGANIZATIONAL CONTEXT

As might be expected in view of the diverse activities of personnel in different organizations, the size and structure of the personnel component differs considerably depending on company size, type of industry, and the like. There also are differences from one organization to another in the decision-making authority and level of responsibility of the personnel staff, as well as differences in training and experience requirements. All these variables are relevant for the person working in a personnel job.

The Personnel Department

In most organizations the personnel staff is relatively small compared to such departments as marketing or manufacturing. Indeed, until a firm reaches a certain size, in terms of number of employees, there usually is no separate personnel department at all. Matters relating to staffing are handled in very small organizations by a top executive with responsibility for several functions; sometimes it is the company president who takes care of all personnel problems.

As a firm grows, the first step toward a formalized personnel function usually is the appointment of a full-time assistant to the president or general manager. One study indicates that this may happen when a company reaches anywhere from 50 to 300 employees, although the average is just over 100 employees. The next step, a staff specialist plus clerical assistance, occurs with 100 to 400 employees, but around the 200-employee level in the majority of companies.

In large organizations, separate personnel staffs may appear at several levels—usually the plant or departmental level, divisional level, and corporate level. A report by the National Industrial Conference Board (NICB) on the personnel structure of 249 companies with 1,000 employees or more indicates that 80 percent have multilevel personnel structures. The structure of the staff is likely to be quite different at each level. The personnel group for a manufacturing plant, for example, might have separate sections for employment, labor relations, training, wages and benefits, and safety and health. At the corporate staff level, sections may be designated only for such areas as organization planning, manpower planning, manpower development, compensation, and personnel research. Of the corporate-level units reported by NICB, most have between 15 and 40 people, and their primary functions are to provide top management with advice on personnel policies and to provide various services to other groups in the company. Even at this level there seems to be little agreement on how the personnel function should be structured. Of the 119 companies that supplied NICB with organization charts, no two were exactly alike.

A few companies split the employee relations function into two completely separate departments. The usual split is between personnel and industrial relations, with the latter department responsible for handling relations with unions; both departments report directly to a top executive. According to a 1970 BNA survey, however, only 5 percent of the responding firms did not have a single top administrator in charge of all personnel and industrial relations activities.

Organizational Status of Personnel—Just as the personnel staff usually is smaller than other organizational groups, the personnel department often has been of relatively low status. There are many indications now that this is changing, that the personnel function is being upgraded, particularly in large corporations. One survey shows that the percentage of corporate personnel vice presidents rose from 28 percent in 1959 to 37 percent in 1969. In smaller firms, top personnel officers at the vice president level are rarer. Among the organizations represented on BNA's *Personnel Policies Forum* (PPF) with less than 1,000 employees, only 7 percent have a personnel or industrial relations vice president, while 26 percent of those with 1,000 employees or more do.

Compensation levels of the top personnel executives also indicate that this field is moving up relatively faster than other areas of management. A report on executive compensation in 1969 indicates an average annual salary for top personnel officers of $34,000, compared to $28,000 in 1959. The average increase was larger than that for top executives in marketing, manufacturing, engineering, and purchasing, or for executive vice presidents.

Personnel Ratios—One measure of the relative importance of personnel within an organization is the personnel ratio, or the number of personnel-industrial relations staff people per hundred employees served. Studies of these ratios have been conducted periodically since 1948 by the University of Minnesota's Industrial Relations Center, under the direction of Dale Yoder. Yoder's most recent survey, conducted in 1970 with the cooperation of the American Society for Personnel Administration (ASPA), shows a ratio of 0.49 professional and technical personnel staff members per hundred employees and a ratio of 1.20 for total personnel staff, including clerical and other supportive employees.

Another measure reported by Yoder is the functional personnel ratio, which shows how the personnel staff time is allocated among different activities. The 1970 results, as reported in the November-December 1970 issue of *The Personnel Administrator*, are shown in the following table:

Functional Personnel Ratios

Function	Percent of Professional Technical Staff Time
Staffing	32.6
Wage and salary administration	14.2
Benefits and services	12.3
Training-development	10.9
Labor relations	9.8
Manpower planning	5.3
Communications	5.3
Employee equal opportunity programs	3.9
Organization planning	3.7
Research	2.0

A comparison of the 1970 survey with earlier ones indicates some of the changes that have occurred in the overall personnel function over time. In 1953, for example, the second highest amount of personnel staff time (nearly one third) was devoted to employee health and safety programs, which do not even appear as a separate category in 1970; presumably these programs are included under benefits and services. As would be expected, employee equal opportunity programs were not mentioned in the 1953 survey.

All these ratios are based on overall averages for all employers responding to the surveys and may not be particularly relevant as far as any one firm is concerned. A more detailed breakdown shows that certain factors tend to influence the personnel ratio. These include—

Size—In general, the larger the operation, the lower the ratio (the fewer personnel staff per 100 employees).

Type of establishment—Single plants have the highest ratios, followed by one plant in a multiplant operation, all plants in a multiplant operation, and finally corporate offices.

Type of industry—Highest ratios are found in public utilities, second highest in banking, finance, and insurance, then manufacturing, government, transportation, and trade lowest.

Location—Highest region is the northwest, followed by the north-central, northeast, southeast, southwest and south-central.

Authority and Responsibility of the Personnel Department

Over the years a major concern among those who have studied personnel management is the authority and responsibility accorded the personnel manager and his department. In most organizations personnel is considered a staff function established primarily to service line management, providing advice and skilled assistance in matters relating to hiring, training, and other aspects of employee relations. Often it is viewed by lower-level line managers with suspicion and fear; personnel people are viewed as trying to undermine their authority.

The line managers' suspicions are not entirely unreasonable. A number of studies show that the difference between "advice" and "decision-making" on the part of personnel managers is minimal in many instances. In one such study many personnel directors defined their role as that of providing advice, assistance, and counsel to line management when in fact they were actually making the decisions for the line managers.

Line managers are not the only ones with whom the personnel staff deals in making decisions; others throughout the management hierarchy may be involved as well. An example of the number of different people involved is provided by the case of one member of BNA's *Personnel Policies Forum*, the director of employee relations of a meatpacking company with nearly 5,000 employees. In response to a survey on the personnel department, he indicated that he shared responsibility for various activities as shown in the table on next page.

However, the fact that the responsibility for any particular matter is shared with some other manager does not say how much authority the personnel manager actually has; it merely indicates that decisions in these areas have to be agreed upon by two or more people. It is probable that in many instances one party or the other actually makes most of the decisions, especially if expert knowledge resides with a particular person. Thus, while decision-making *re-*

Decision-Making Authority of a Personnel Executive

Responsibility Shared With	In Administration of These Activities
Top Management	Planning general personnel policies Manpower planning Organization planning Vacations and holidays Military and other leaves
Salary Committee	Nonmanagement pay policies Executive compensation
Industrial Engineering	Incentive pay
Company Insurance Department	Group Insurance* Pensions* Health and medical services
Public Relations Department Employee Organization Line Supervisors	Community Relations Recreation and social activities Recruiting and selection Performance appraisal Promotion, transfer, and separation Induction, orientation, and on-the-job training Supervisory training and management development Educational and scholarship programs Job evaluation Employee counseling Discipline and grievance handling Safety and working conditions Housing and moving services Union relations

* These functions shared also with the Corporate Secretary and top management.

sponsibility may be shared in many areas, the real *authority* is not necessarily shared.

Level of Responsibility.—The real authority of a personnel manager usually is related to the level of responsibility accorded to the personnel function in a particular organizational unit. Four levels of responsibility can be described as follows:

Lowest level—personnel work consists of processing paperwork and keeping records on employees and job applicants.

Second level—personnel staff is concerned with interpersonal relations and acts as a communications link between higher management and lower level employees.

Third level—personnel sets up systems and procedures for hiring, training, performance appraisal, and so forth and monitors to make sure the systems are working.

Highest level—personnel provides expertise on broad policy questions relating to human-resources management.

The two highest levels are most likely to be found in division-wide or corporate personnel structures. In any one personnel unit, however, there may be different levels of responsibility related to different activities. A plant personnel department, for example, may have only the lowest level responsibility with respect to wage and salary administration, merely recording wage changes of employees that are decided upon at a higher level. In the training area, the same personnel department may be charged with the determination of training needs and the planning, implementing, and evaluation of several programs—a third-level responsibility. While the level of responsibility may be a direct function of company size and type, it often depends in large measure on the influence the top personnel executive has developed over the years. How influential he becomes depends in turn on his relationship with the chief executive of the organization and on the confidence management in general has in his knowledge, capability, and effectiveness.

People in Personnel

A factor related to the personnel executive's influence in the organization is that for many years the image of the personnel man in all but the largest companies was that all that was needed to do the job was a pleasant personality and the ability to get along with people. The major role was viewed as that of keeping employees "happy," by whatever means possible, rather than that of managing human resources to contribute to organizational goals. Increasingly, however, this image is changing, and people in personnel are adopting a more professional approach to their jobs.

As in all areas of management, more and more men and women entering the field of personnel are expected to have a college education, preferably with a degree in business administration or management. College courses related to personnel that are taken most frequently by those who later become personnel managers include industrial psychology, personnel administration, labor relations, and human relations. Courses relevant to all aspects of management, such as the newer courses in organization theory and behavior, also have been recommended to those interested in personnel careers.

In relatively small organizational units, such as those at the plant level, and in the very highest personnel positions, such as corporate vice president, broad general training and experience in addition to a business education provide the best background. Many companies give all their managers a year or two in personnel to demonstrate how the personnel department can help them when they are back in line management. Similarly, many personnel executives advise young people interested in careers in personnel to get some experience in line supervision along the way, to learn at first hand the types of problems encountered in managing a group of employees.

Besides those with broad business or generalized personnel backgrounds, in any large organization you will find a diverse group of people working on one aspect or another of personnel. Lawyers handle labor relations, doctors staff company medical facilities, educators set up training programs, psychologists administer testing procedures and conduct research studies, journalists prepare employee publications, engineers supervise safety standards, accountants review employee benefit payments. Beginning jobs in particular may require some specialized background or training.

The relative impact of each of these professions or disciplines varies over time and with differing circumstances within and outside the organization. In the next chapter, which traces the history of the field since the beginning of this century, we shall see how the various specialized areas have influenced the development of personnel management and contributed to its present status in the world of management.

CHAPTER 2

The Evolution of Personnel Management

To provide some understanding of how personnel management evolved to its present position within the broader area of general management, we shall take a look at the historical development of the field over the past century. Each of the myriad activities and responsibilities of the personnel department has been affected by outside influences—sometimes as a result of new knowledge from such disciplines as sociology, psychology, engineering, or accounting; more often due to economic and social forces, especially as they are reflected in governmental actions.

As might be anticipated from the fact that outside forces have had such a profound effect on the development of personnel management, its evolution has been anything but continous and steady. At least until recent years, personnel has experienced great spurts of growth at some points in time while at other times it has suffered tremendous setbacks to the point of practically disappearing from the industrial scene. At the present time, personnel appears to be firmly enough established to function even during times of financial crisis. Although many personnel activities may be curtailed when a company has to cut back its work force, only the very smallest firms eliminate the personnel department altogether.

Two sets of conflicting trends have characterized and at times hindered the development of personnel management over the years. One of these involves the conflict between the approach taken by economists, accountants, and industrial engineers on the one hand, and the approach of those who take what is called the social welfare point of view on the other. With the former, the emphasis is on managing human resources so as to achieve maximum contribution to profit or productivity, while the latter are concerned primarily with employee satisfaction. In terms of the organizational

17

goals described in Chapter 1, the first group tends to emphasize the productivity goal to the exclusion of the maintenance goal, and those in the social welfare tradition do just the opposite.

The second conflicting trend is that of the relationship of personnel to the line managers throughout the organization—the line-staff conflict, also mentioned in Chapter 1. As we point out in the following discussion, there have been times when many personnel departments had virtually no decision-making authority at all, and other times when personnel people were given authority to make most, if not all, decisions relating to such processes as hiring and firing. The trend back and forth in this regard has been strongly influenced by economic, social, and political forces, whereas the social welfare-profitability conflict has been influenced most by the results of scientific research.

THE EARLY PERIOD

Scholars with an academic interest in the philosophy underlying personnel management have traced its origins back as far as such ancient writers as Plato, but for our purposes the advent of the industrial revolution marks the earliest period of interest. It was not until business organizations were of large enough size to warrant managerial departmentalization that a separate personnel function appeared, and personnel usually was the last to appear as a department. During the last quarter of the nineteenth century, a number of companies established separate departments to handle finance and accounting, production, and marketing, but it was not until after the turn of the century that full-scale departments devoted to the personnel function were established. However, there were some developments during this period that did have an impact on personnel management. We shall mention these briefly.

Beginnings of the Labor Movement

Of all the social forces operating in the United States during the nineteenth century, the emergence of the organized labor movement had the greatest effect on the development of personnel management. A few trade unions, mostly in skilled crafts and on a strictly local level, date back to the 1780s and '90s, but it was not until 100 years later that any lasting national group of labor unions was formed. One famous, but unsuccessful, attempt to unite various unions under one umbrella was the Noble Order of the Knights of Labor, founded in 1869 and reported to have had some 700,000 members at its height. In 1886, a number of dissatisfied leaders of the Knights of Labor joined with another small group of unions that had banded together five years earlier and formed the American Federation of Labor (AFL), which became the spokesman for organized labor for the next several decades.

The conflict that led to the demise of the Knights of Labor was a basic philosophical difference between those who viewed the labor union as primarily a means for achieving economic objectives, such as higher wages and better working conditions, and those whose aims were more political, or socialist, in nature. The formation of the AFL represented a victory for the leaders interested solely in economic gains, as personified by its president, Samuel Gompers, known for his statement that the goal of the labor unions was "more." In contrast to the labor movement in many European countries where unions often have demanded and achieved a voice in running industry, American unions generally have followed the Gompers philosophy of letting management run the business, while at the same time trying to increase labor's share in the results. It is because of this emphasis on wages and working conditions that the growth of the union movement has had a major impact on personnel policies but relatively little impact in other areas of management.

Beginnings of Industrial Psychology

The academic discipline that has had the greatest influence on personnel practice as we know it today is that of psychology, which emerged in the late 1800s as a combination of physiology and philosophy. One of the first psychologists to apply the new science to industrial problems was James McKeen Cattell of Columbia University, who is credited with many of the concepts relating to individual differences and psychological testing. By 1890, Cattell had spawned the term *mental test,* and in later years he founded The Psychological Corporation, one of the earliest and largest publishers of psychological tests for industry.

Another early industrial psychologist was Hugo Muensterberg at Harvard University. One of Muensterberg's major contributions to the field was his strong emphasis on empirical analysis and statistical validation, both of which continue to be reflected in personnel research as it is conducted today.

The Welfare Movement

The most relevant aspect of the industrial scene during the post-Civil War years insofar as personnel management is concerned was the welfare movement. During this period many companies adopted programs for improving both the social and the working conditions of their workers. Often employers provided housing, medical care, schools, libraries, and recreational facilities because these were lacking in the community. In some instances the impetus for such programs stemmed from the fact that under the new factory systems there was less employer-employee contact; some employers were responding to criticisms of factory conditions in the popular press; and still others were responding to the threat of the organized labor movement.

To administer these programs larger companies often hired "welfare secretaries," many of whom had a background in social work. The social welfare trend in personnel management comes initially from these welfare secretaries, who on occasion visited workers' homes and furnished financial aid just as today's social welfare workers do. Until the 1900s, the position of welfare secretary appears to have been the only strictly personnel-related position in industry, but this type of welfare movement in the industrial setting began to disappear as the idea of employment or personnel management developed. Before discussing these early personnel departments, and the growth of the field in the early 1900s, however, we will take up another development with origins in the field of industrial engineering, which provided a quite different approach to the utilization of human resources.

Scientific Management

Whereas the work of the welfare secretaries was related almost exclusively to what we now call organizational maintenance considerations, the work of the industrial engineers was concerned with methods for achieving maximum productivity. Called *scientific management,* this movement was supported by such well-known advocates as Frederick W. Taylor and Frank and Lillian Gilbreth. The basic premise behind scientific management is that workers can be induced to attain the highest levels of productivity by the use of scien-

tific selection procedures, appropriate training methods, and monetary incentives. The approach also emphasized the establishment of
ideal physical conditions and work methods.

While the major goal of scientific management was to cut down
on waste by making labor more efficient, it did give important consideration to the welfare of the individual worker on the job. The
worker was to be given training to increase his skill in performing the
job, for example, and he was to be compensated fairly on the basis of
what he produced. In spite of such considerations, the scientific-
management movement was viewed with suspicion and fear by
workers and unions for many years, and the "time-study man"
caught the brunt of much antimanagement sentiment.

The First Personnel Departments

Recognition for the establishment of the first personnel department generally is accorded to John H. Patterson, owner and president of the National Cash Register Company, of Dayton, Ohio. The
first step in the 1890s involved concentrating all the company's welfare activities in one department; in 1902 a Labor Department was
designated with responsibility for employment, handling grievances,
wage administration, improved working conditions, record-keeping,
and training, including "worker improvement." The transition from
a strictly welfare approach to a more productivity-oriented approach
is apparent in the innovations which Patterson introduced, such as a
suggestion system and the provision of monetary rewards on the
basis of individual merit.

Although most early personnel departments were not as comprehensive as NCR's, many other companies did establish similar
programs, usually under the direction of an employment manager.
By 1912, there were enough employment managers to form their
own association. In 1917, when the first national meeting of employment managers was held, there were 10 local associations and more
than 1,000 member companies.

The effect of scientific management on the formation of personnel departments during this period was quite marked. For the approach to be effective, management had to establish and administer
proper selection, training, and compensation programs—all personnel responsibilities. Another impetus to the growth of personnel was
the discovery of the costs of labor turnover around 1913. Studies of
situations where foremen were hiring and firing different workers

nearly every day of the week pointed to high labor costs. Further research by a number of labor economists led to the conclusion that turnover costs could be reduced by improved selection and placement procedures, and this was the basis for the establishment of employment departments in a number of companies.

World War I

Although American involvement in World War I lasted less than two years, this period did produce a significant contribution to the development of the personnel field. On the industrial scene, the impact of the war on personnel activities was felt mostly in the training area, as skilled labor became scarce. It was in the military, however, through the work of psychologists, that one of the most historically significant contributions to personnel management was made.

To help the Army solve the problem of how to decide which of its millions of recruits to train as officers, and which to send to technical training programs, a group of psychologists constructed the first group intelligence test, the Army Alpha. When it became apparent that many recruits were illiterate, another test, the Army Beta, was designed to test the intelligence of those who were not able to read and write. These tests, together with rating systems developed by psychologists for judging candidates for promotion to captain, proved to be very effective and contributed to the efficient utilization of manpower by the Army. Their development provided the foundation for personnel testing and appraisal systems as they exist today.

THE 1920s AND 1930s

The beginning of the decade of the 1920s marked what is probably the bleakest period in the history of personnel. A severe economic depression caused many of the companies with personnel or employment departments to disband them completely, and by 1922 there were so few employment managers left that their annual meeting was cancelled. Starting in 1923, however, personnel management began a comeback, as industry in general experienced rapid expansion in an era of economic prosperity. During the period from 1923 to 1929, personnel activities were undertaken by many employers, although they were not always organized into a formal department.

Also during this period the first textbooks on the subject appeared, several personnel consulting firms were formed, and colleges began to offer courses related to personnel.

The Age of Paternalism

Employee welfare, in the form of a large variety of benefits and services, was a major characteristic of personnel management during the 1920s. In some companies, the administration of benefit plans was all the personnel department handled, and in others the only personnel activity conducted on a formal basis was the medical department. In effect, the company doctor or nurse *was* the personnel manager. The medical department often had responsibility for employee safety, which assumed increasing importance with the newly enacted state workmen's compensation laws.

The motives behind these personnel programs were not entirely paternalistic. A major factor was management's concern about the growth of union membership, which had been encouraged by government policies during World War I. According to one observer, the introduction of so many employee benefit programs during the 1920s resulted in the labor movement's being "killed by kindness."

While membership in national unions did decrease from 1923 to 1929, company unions, often called "work councils" or "shop committees," became particularly widespread. These groups usually were sponsored by management, and in some cases their responsibilities were limited to such activities as planning the company picnic. However, they appear to have been effective deterrents to outside unionization of employees.

Personnel's Changing Role

Increasing conflict over the role of personnel in the organization was another characteristic of the 1920s. In many companies, the personnel function had begun with the appointment of an employment manager to take over the responsibilities of hiring and firing from the work group foremen. Thus the employment manager was given authority to make decisions for line management in an effort to reduce turnover or to make selection more "scientific." The line supervisors resented what they felt was interference with their responsibility for handling these personnel functions insofar as their own employees were concerned, and many campaigned hard to have this decision-making authority restored. The proper role for personnel, they asserted, was that of a staff function operating in an advisory capacity to line managers, at least as far as any actions related to their own subordinates were concerned.

This viewpoint led to a vote in 1923 by the National Personnel Association (successor to the National Association of Employment Managers) to change its name to the American Management Association. Reasons given for the change included the view that line managers must deal directly with their personnel responsibilities and that personnel could not be treated as an isolated function. As a result of this action the personnel department assumed more and more of a staff role, although it still had decision-making authority over specified activities such as the administration of employee benefits.

The Hawthorne Studies

A series of studies that have had a substantial impact on the field of personnel management began at the end of the 1920s and extended over several years. These were the Hawthorne studies, a series of experiments conducted at the Hawthorne plant of the Western Electric Company near Chicago. The initial purpose of the experiments was to determine the effects of various physical factors such as light and ventilation on worker productivity. As the studies progressed, however, it became apparent that emotional and motivational factors had more effect on productivity than did physical factors. Particularly important were the worker's relationships with others in the work group and the amount and kind of attention received from superiors.

The results of the Hawthorne studies have been widely cited and led to what became known as the human relations movement in industry. For many people in personnel, the findings seemed to support their theory that "a happy employee is a productive employee"—a theory which was used to justify many of the large-scale employee welfare programs of the 1920s. Thus the Hawthorne studies provided scientific legitimacy to the social welfare tradition within personnel. However, their major influence on the field was delayed until after the Great Depression, when the country was in the midst of a wartime economy.

The Depression

From the experience of personnel during the depression period of 1921 and 1922, it might be anticipated that the much longer depression of the 1930s would have had an even more adverse effect. This was not the case, however. At least, personnel departments did not disappear entirely, although most of them were reduced in size as many of their activities were curtailed. A large number of the liberal employee benefit programs of the previous decade were discontinued in cost-cutting efforts, and many profit-sharing and stock-purchase programs were abandoned as worthless.

One effect of the depression on the activities of the personnel department in at least some large companies was to place more emphasis on research-oriented programs such as job analysis and employee attitude surveys, in efforts to utilize human resources more effectively. Some companies underwent a complete organizational restructuring; others revamped their wage and salary policies entirely. The welfare tradition in personnel clearly took a back seat during this period, and there was a strong shift to justifying personnel programs in terms of their contribution to productivity and profit. However, the most significant development for personnel management during the 1930s did not stem directly from the depression. It was the result of legislation passed at the federal level, much of it aimed at boosting economic recovery.

Effects of Social Legislation

Beginning with the passage of the Norris-LaGuardia Act of 1932, Congress enacted a series of laws that had a profound effect on personnel management; for the first time unions were provided governmental support in their organizing efforts. The Norris-LaGuardia Act made it much more difficult for employers to get court injunctions to prevent work stoppages, and it also made unenforceable so-called yellow-dog contracts, under which workers agreed when they were hired that they would not join a union. Both these devices had been widely used by employers to discourage union membership, and they undoubtedly were a major reason for the slow growth of labor unions during the 1920s.

The most important legislation passed during this period was the 1935 National Labor Relations Act (Wagner Act), which stated that it was the government's purpose to actively encourage the growth of trade unions and to restrain management from interfering with this growth in any way. The Act also guaranteed workers the right to bargain collectively with their employers over wages and working conditions and established the National Labor Relations Board (NLRB) to

administer the law and investigate complaints of unfair labor practices. Given this positive legal climate, union membership grew from
less than three million in 1933 to 8.6 million by 1941 and a new type of
union, the industrial union, emerged. Most of the early unions that
formed the American Federation of Labor were organized on a craft
basis and included only workers in a single occupation; the industrial unions included all types of workers in a given industry, regardless of specific occupation. They began membership drives in a number of industries that had never been unionized before, such as
automobiles and rubber. Initially these unions were established
within the AFL, but increasing conflicts of interest with the craft
unions led to their seceding from the AFL in 1935 and forming the
Congress of Industrial Organizations (CIO).

This new union strength stimulated both growth in personnel
management and a change in its direction. Many companies that had
not previously had a formal personnel program introduced one in
hopes of heading off union organizing attempts, while some employers found themselves faced with the necessity of establishing a
personnel department, or at least appointing a management representative, to deal with the union. It was during this period that labor
relations and industrial relations became common designations for
the company unit handling these matters, and labor lawyers became
part of the personnel scene as employers endeavored to keep their
old prerogatives and still stay within the new laws.

One result was that line management found itself losing much
of the authority and responsibility in personnel matters that it had
gained during the period of the 1920s. Many areas of supervisory decision-making authority, particularly with regard to hiring and firing,
were now subject to legal constraints. The traditional responsibilities
were now being centralized in the personnel or labor relations office
to make sure the terms of the collective bargaining agreement were
followed. Increasingly, the personnel department found itself concerned with developing strategies for keeping the union out or for
negotiating and administering the labor agreement with a minimum
of conflict should a union succeed in organizing the employees.

WORLD WAR II

As in World War I, personnel research conducted by the military
during World War II on the use of various selection and appraisal

techniques resulted in lasting contributions to the personnel field. However, the major impact of World War II on personnel management was much more direct; because of the huge scale and tremendous manpower resources involved in conducting the war, the Federal Government assumed control of many aspects of the personnel function in the private sector. This was achieved through the work of two special governmental units—the War Manpower Commission and the War Labor Board.

The War Manpower Commission

The role of the War Manpower Commission was to plan programs for most effectively utilizing the nation's manpower, to locate and allocate the people and skills needed by the military, civilian government agencies, industry, and agriculture. The Commission encouraged companies to develop manning tables, or manpower inventories, and replacement schedules that would point up hiring and training needs. For most companies, this was their first introduction to the concept of manpower planning on a long-range basis.

It was in the training area that the work of the Commission had the most lasting effects on personnel management. A major task that had to be accomplished was to train in a short period of time the large numbers of individuals, many of them women with no previous employment experience, who came to work in the defense plants. In many instances, the people doing the training had no prior experience as instructors. The Training Within Industry division of the Commission conducted a series of Job Instruction Training (JIT) sessions that proved highly successful in training the trainers. The guidelines developed in these programs were used in industrial skill-training programs and are the basis of much of today's on-the-job training.

Another type of program stimulated by the Commission was university training for higher level managers and executives. The government was responsible for the establishment of the Advanced Management Program at Harvard in 1943. Under another government program, management-development courses on one topic or another were offered by more than 200 colleges and universities during the wartime period. Before this time, very few companies provided any type of training other than for employees involved in a formal apprenticeship program. As a result of the World War II em-

phasis, training and development became a standard personnel activity, and many companies now have large staffs of training specialists with backgrounds in industrial education.

The War Labor Board

As far as industry was concerned, the Manpower Commission
operated mostly in an advisory capacity, whereas the War Labor
Board had direct authority over private employers in two major areas
of personnel—wage and salary administration and labor relations.
When the United States entered World War II, there still was considerable labor unrest as the unions continued their large-scale organizing efforts. The War Labor Board was established to stabilize wartime wages in order to prevent disputes, to settle any disputes over
wages that did occur without the loss of production, and to help
settle disputes involving rival unions claiming representation of the
same group of workers. Such jurisdictional controversy had become
increasingly common as a result of the growth of the CIO.

In the area of wage and salary administration, the War Labor
Board had authority over employers, whether there was any union
involved or not. All employers, except those with very few employees, were subject to the regulations set forth by the Board limiting
the amount of wage increases and stipulating the circumstances under which other types of wage adjustments could and could not be
made. One result was that companies increasingly offered extra payments, or fringe benefits, such as paid holidays and vacations, which
the Board generally approved. These were offered either as induce-
ments to attract employees or under the pressure of demands from
unions, which were prevented from bargaining for higher wages and
wanted something "more" to show their members as a result of their
negotiating efforts.

The wage stabilization program had a major effect on wage and
salary administration in industry. As in the training area, the majority
of companies had no formal personnel unit engaged in wage and
salary administration before World War II. In order to keep up with
the War Labor Board's orders and regulations and make sure they
were being followed, such units became common. Companies that
had previously established plans for job evaluation, wage progression, and other formal wage administration practices were permitted
to make adjustments in accordance with these plans without prior
approval. This led to the adoption of more formal wage and salary

administration systems both during and after the war. Two concepts introduced by the Board that still underly wage and salary administration are tying wage decisions to changes in the cost of living and the use of wage-survey data as the basis for adjusting inequities in the rates paid by one company as compared to another.

Overall, World War II saw the number and importance of the activities handled by the personnel department grow rapidly. The role of the personnel manager became much more visible in the organization as he became involved in matters of manpower utilization and government regulation that were of concern at the highest management levels. Even though personnel was still viewed as a staff function, most personnel departments took over many more of the line supervisors' responsibilities during this period. This was in part to make sure laws and government regulations were complied with, in part because supervisors were concentrating their efforts on maximizing production for the wartime economy, in part because many of the supervisors were new in that role and thus grateful for all the help they could get from the personnel department, and in part because of continued pressures from the unions.

THE POSTWAR ERA

By the end of World War II, the major components of the personnel function as we know it today were well established, and the nearly 50-year period of rapid and often dramatic changes in the field—both up and down—came to at least a temporary end. For the next 20 years, the changes in personnel management were evolutionary rather than revolutionary, and growth occurred by the extension of existing concepts and practices to smaller and different types of organizations rather than by the creation of whole new areas of jurisdiction for the personnel department.

In the period immediately following the war, personnel management did have to cope with some new problems relating to government regulation, such as veterans' reemployment rights. Shortly afterward, in the early 1950s, wage and salary controls again were imposed by the government to provide economic stabilization during the Korean conflict. The immediate postwar period also witnessed a rash of extended strikes, many of them related to union demands for expansion of health and welfare programs, retirement plans, and other fringe benefits that were becoming increasingly costly to management. This situation led to the passage of the Taft-Hartley Act in 1947, which restored to management some of the power it lost under the Wagner Act. Despite Taft-Hartley, unions continued to prosper in this period, growing from nearly 13 million members in 1945 to over 17 million by 1954. The political power of the labor movement was strengthened in 1955 when the major federations merged to form the AFL-CIO. The merger did not, however, result in any immediate reduction in the number of jurisdictional disputes causing problems for management. Thus, both the labor-relations and government-relations aspects of personnel management continued to be areas of major concern.

Adding to the difficulties created by union and governmental pressures, increasing demands for skilled manpower, particularly in the technical and engineering occupations, required new approaches by the personnel department. During the 1950s extensive college-recruiting programs were undertaken by most large corporations in an effort to cope with manpower shortages. The technological advances of this period produced a variety of problems in human resource utilization that did not seem to lend themselves to easy solution by the traditional personnel techniques. Increasingly, management began looking to the academic world for possible answers to its manpower problems. And increasingly, since the end of World War II, academic resources and the interest of academicians have been directed to questions relating to human resource management in organizations.

The Expanded Role of the University

Within the university community there were two developments in the postwar period that contributed to the expansion and sophistication of personnel management. The first of these was a marked increase in the number of courses dealing with various aspects of the personnel function being offered at both undergraduate and graduate levels, as well as the establishment of personnel management as a major field of study in most collegiate schools of business administration.

The second development was the large number of research centers and institutes devoted to the study of manpower problems that were established after the war. University-related personnel research units go back as far as 1915 at Carnegie Institute of Technology and to 1922 at Princeton, where the Industrial Relations section of the Economics Department was created with the support of Rockefeller money. During the 1930s, industrial relations centers were established at the University of Michigan, Stanford, MIT, and California Institute of Technology. Nearly all these pre-World War II institutions were supported by resources outside the universities themselves, however. During the 1940s and 1950s nearly 50 such research centers came into being, many of them supported by university or public funds, and some of them offering degree programs in personnel and industrial relations. Among the most prominent of these programs are those of the New York State School of Industrial and Labor Relations established at Cornell University in 1944, the Institute of Labor and Industrial Relations at the University of Illinois in 1946, and the Industrial Relations Center at the University of Minnesota in 1945.

The university industrial relations centers have attracted and provided expert training to large numbers of individuals in the personnel field, both practitioners and those who continue to pursue an academic career. Participating in the work of the institutes have been economists, psychologists, sociologists, industrial engineers, political scientists, and lawyers. Their research efforts represent a significant contribution to basic knowledge in the field, bringing to bear the perspective of many disciplines. Personnel research also is conducted by private organizations and a number of large corporations, some of which established personnel research units back in the 1920s when they introduced large-scale testing and appraisal programs. For many years, however, the findings from company research efforts were not made available outside the organization, so the contribution to our general knowledge was negligible. With the increased emphasis at the university level and the support for academic research on manpower utilization problems, the theories relating to personnel matters that have been advanced and tested have mushroomed. While few final solutions have been discovered, the work of the academics, particularly the behavioral scientists, has led to new approaches for the personnel practitioner.

Behavioral Science Research

As noted, behavioral science research in industry, at least on a small scale, goes back to the 1920s. The majority of these early research projects were conducted by psychologists and were concerned with aspects of psychological measurement—testing, rating systems, attitude surveys, job analysis, and the like. The first major effort by psychologists and sociologists at studying the dynamics of work groups and the effectiveness of leadership techniques grew out of the Hawthorne studies of the late 1920s. These experiments seemed to indicate that the more permissive supervisor was more effective than the one who was highly authoritarian. But it was not until the World War II period that these studies had any widespread impact in industry.

Another series of studies, conducted by Kurt Lewin and others at the University of Iowa, seemed to support the Hawthorne conclusions, although the Iowa research did not take place in an industrial setting. On the basis of these and other studies, the postwar period saw the introduction of large numbers of supervisory training and management development programs with a heavy emphasis on human relations courses. This approach was fostered by the welfare approach in personnel, in that the training programs stressed the importance of kindness and consideration in dealing with subordinates. The productivity goal also would be furthered by this approach, it was argued, because employees who were more satisfied with their work situation would perform more effectively and thus contribute more to the company's productivity and profits.

Over the decade of the 1950s a vast amount of behavioral science research was directed at the employee satisfaction-performance relationship as it became increasingly clear that the human relations approach did not always result in increased productivity; in fact, it sometimes had just the opposite result. The evidence indicated that the long-accepted assumption of a constant, positive relationship between job satisfaction and work output was basically incorrect. The studies overall showed no evidence for a consistent relationship of any kind. Also during the 1950s personnel researchers were developing evidence that many of the personnel techniques that had been used for many years, such as the selection interview, were less effective than had been assumed. The behavioral scientists seemed to be raising many more questions than they were answering; it became obvious that much more research into these problems was needed.

The 1960s experienced a tremendous amount of personnel and organizational research in both the academic and the business environment, and company researchers were publishing more and more of their results, to the benefit of the entire field. One new approach involved viewing the business organization as a system and working from the top down to effect change. This evolved from the observation that the first-level supervisor often was put into a conflict position after human-relations-type training if his own superiors were still operating on an authoritarian basis. The overall emphasis began to change from one of trying to find ways of "satisfying" employees to achieving results that contribute to organizational goals. The result for personnel management was that policies and practices relating to human resource utilization increasingly could be based on scientific research as to their effectiveness in a specific company.

The Move Toward Professionalization

For personnel practice itself, a significant development over the past 20 to 25 years has been the move to a more professional occupation. Both the expansion of university work in personnel and private research efforts have contributed to this movement. It is doubtful that personnel practice will achieve the full professional status of such areas as medicine, law, psychology, or accounting, partly because many personnel practitioners already are in one of these other professional fields. However, there is an increasing sense of professional identity among those in personnel and increasing concern over matters of ethical personnel practice. Two facets of the move toward professionalization are the growth of personnel associations and the proliferation of periodicals and scientific journals in the field.

Personnel Associations—From 1923, when the National Personnel Association turned into the American Management Association (AMA) until the formation of the American Society for Personnel Administration (ASPA) in 1948, there was no national, comprehensive professional association for people in all types of organizations interested in all aspects of personnel management. The AMA did, and still does, sponsor many local and national seminars and workshops in various aspects of personnel, but it also is concerned with marketing, production, finance, and the other areas of general management. There also are many associations for those with primary interest in safety, training, or other components of the overall personnel function as well as many general personnel associations based on geographical or industry jurisdictions. One fairly general personnel association, the Society for Personnel Administration

(SPA), appeared in the 1930s, but its membership has been strongly oriented toward personnel operations in the Federal Government and other public institutions. In January 1973, SPA merged with the Public Personnel Association (PPA), which includes many state and local public personnel officers. This new association, the International Personnel Management Association, clearly reflects the recent growth in personnel, and particularly in labor relations, activities in the public sector.

From its founding in Ohio with a membership of 92 individuals in 1948, the ASPA has grown to include close to 10,000 members in all 50 states and 14 foreign countries. Much of its growth has come through the affiliation of well-established local and regional personnel groups. Among the professional activities sponsored by the ASPA, in addition to regular local and national conferences, are the funding of research projects by graduate students and professors and the development of a code of ethics for personnel administrators.

Two other groups, although of more limited membership than ASPA, have contributed much in the way of knowledge and professional prestige to the field. The first of these, the Industrial Relations Research Association (IRRA), was formed in 1947 by a group of labor relations practitioners, mostly economists in the academic world. Its membership has grown to include representatives from the government and private industry, although its research interests have been concentrated primarily on union relations and matters of broad economic problems, such as manpower planning and utilization on a national level.

The second group is Division 14 of the American Psychological Association (APA). From 1937 until 1945 Division 14 was the American Association of Applied Psychology. With its admission to APA, it became the Business and Industrial Division, later shortened to Industrial only, and in 1970 it was changed to Division of Industrial and Organizational Psychology to indicate the broad-gauge interests of its members. Division 14 includes in its membership personnel researchers from the nation's major corporations and the government as well as most academics working in the area, and its annual meetings have afforded an opportunity for the results of this research to be widely disseminated.

Periodicals in Personnel—Two of the best known periodicals in the field date back to the early 1920s. These are *Personnel,* published

bimonthly by AMA, and the monthly *Personnel Journal,* which began as the *Journal of Personnel Research* and is published privately.
Also dating back to this period are various publications and reports
of the National Industrial Conference Board (NICB), a research
group representing a number of private companies and associations.
In 1937 NICB began its series of "Studies in Personnel Policy," which
has provided survey data on numerous personnel practices over the
years. Also in 1937, the Society for Personnel Administration began
to publish *Personnel Administration,* a bimonthly journal for its
members and others "interested in sound management."

Several other journals and magazines that have been published
for many years often include articles pertinent to personnel although their focus generally is broader. In this category are *Journal
of Applied Psychology,* published by APA; *Management Review,* an
AMA publication; *Monthly Labor Review,* published by the U.S. Department of Labor; and *Harvard Business Review.*

Since World War II several new periodicals in the field have appeared, some in conjunction with the new university research centers. Thus, the Cornell School of Industrial and Labor Relations in
1947 began the quarterly *Industrial and Labor Relations Review,*
which has a strong emphasis on labor problems and collective bargaining. In 1961 the Institute of Industrial Relations at the University
of California began publishing *Industrial Relations: A Journal of
Economy and Society,* which covers "all aspects of the employment
relationship, with special attention to developments in labor economics, sociology, psychology, political science, and law."

In the behavioral sciences there are also several newer journals.
One of the most notable for personnel management is *Personnel
Psychology,* published quarterly since 1948 "to stimulate and report
the application of psychological methods, understandings, techniques, and findings to personnel problems." A number of national
associations began issuing regular publications during this period,
and shortly after its founding ASPA began its bimonthly magazine
The Personnel Administrator.

While our discussion provides some idea of the growth of personnel literature, it is impossible to mention all the periodicals covering one or more aspects of personnel. An indication of this is found
in a 1971 BNA survey in which personnel executives were asked to
list the professional periodicals they read regularly; among the 100
respondents, a total of 133 different periodicals were mentioned.

RECENT DEVELOPMENTS

The major postwar developments resulted in greatly increased knowledge and academic interest in personnel, but no basic changes occurred in personnel practice as a direct consequence of either academic or professional activities. While behavioral scientists theorized over the employee satisfaction-motivation-productivity relationship, personnel staffers and line managers in many organizations continued to be in conflict over who has authority over what personnel decisions. This is not to say the field did not change at all between the mid-1940s and the mid-1960s; as we have indicated, the number and size of personnel departments did grow and the whole approach to personnel became more professional.

A 1966 NICB study of large companies revealed the nature of some of the changes that had taken place in the personnel function over the previous decade. In about half the 249 firms surveyed, the personnel staff had grown faster than the company's overall work force, and in most of them the top personnel executive was a vice president, indicating that the level of personnel titles and reporting relationships had moved up. In contrast to the early 1950s, when labor relations was the top concern in personnel, the major focus in the mid-1960s was on management development, organization and manpower planning, employee benefits, and personnel research.

Since about the mid-1960s, personnel has found itself more and more at the center of "the action" in management. The rapidly changing values of society in the past few years have resulted in many segments of the population demanding that organizations, particularly business organizations, concern themselves with the good of society as well as the good of the company. The government has assumed an expanding role in pressing all our institutions—educational as well as industrial—to act in accordance with these changing values.

Such legislation as the Civil Rights Act of 1964 has created major changes in personnel management. Top management increasingly looks to the personnel department for solutions to the problems of complying with legal requirements with a minimum of disruption and cost. And it is increasingly clear that personnel decision-making and information-handling need to be centralized within the organization to make sure policies required by the laws are being effectively carried out.

Again, we find economic as well as social forces having a very marked effect on the field of personnel management. The government's wage control program, prompted by inflation and high unemployment, brought personnel even more to the forefront of management concern, and in the process contributed to the difficulty of personnel decision-making.

Almost all the elements of personnel practice have been affected to some degree by the changes in the past few years as the legal influences on personnel decision-making have increased. In the next chapter we will consider these influences and others of a nonlegal nature that serve to define what is possible in trying to achieve effective utilization of human resources.

CHAPTER 3

Influences on Personnel Decisions

Up to this point we have provided a general definition of personnel management and examined its historical development. Now we consider another aspect of the field that will afford added perspective before moving to the more detailed discussion of specific personnel activities in Part II. Our concern is with the various factors that influence personnel decisions. Some of these factors aid decisions by pointing to a course of action which *should* be taken to accomplish a goal most effectively; other factors, especially those with legal implications, indicate action which *can or cannot* be taken. Because both types of factors have a direct influence on personnel policies and practices, it is important to be aware of them, and to have current information on their implications.

There are a number of factors both inside and outside the organization that can affect personnel planning in a general way. These are factors relating to the characteristics of the work force and to the outside environment which need to be taken into account in making long-range decisions. Differences in age, intelligence, and abilities of employees may indicate whether a major expansion requiring a large number of new managers is feasible. Cultural and geographical characteristics also can affect decisions relating to human resources management. A company facility that calls for considerable high-talent manpower, such as a research and development center, will be much better located near a cultural and educational center than in the middle of the prairies. Factors such as these should be of major concern to top management in planning for the future, and for personnel management in its daily operations. A plant that *is* located out in the prairies, for example, is likely to require more in the way of employee services such as feeding and medical care than one in a metropolitan area.

Of even greater influence on the daily operation of the personnel department are the various laws, at the local, state, and national level, that regulate an increasing number of personnel activities. Because of the vast number of laws that have some bearing on managerial decisions relating to the utilization of human resources, it is not possible to provide a comprehensive catalog here. However, we will discuss those laws that have had the greatest impact on personnel management.

LEGAL INFLUENCES

Legislation related to employment matters goes back to the early 1800s at the state and local level, when there was widespread concern over child labor and factory working conditions in general. As indicated in Chapter 2, however, the advent of such legislation on a national level is relatively recent, and it was not until the 1930s that the Federal Government moved to regulate personnel activities on any large scale. The depression-era legislation affected primarily labor relations, wages and hours, and the payment of social security and unemployment compensation benefits. Federal regulation in the personnel domain was largely confined to these areas until the mid-1960s, although during periods of economic controls the government has exercised much more direct influence.

Over the past decade the impact of regulation by the Federal Government has grown tremendously. Contributing to this growth were the passage of the Civil Rights Act of 1964, the enactment of the Occupational Safety and Health Act of 1970, and the imposition of wage and salary controls in 1971. Also contributing has been the extension of existing federal laws to cover types of organizations not previously within their jurisdiction and to include much smaller employing units. For example, when the Civil Rights Act went into effect in 1965, the employment provisions applied to firms of 100 or more employees. Coverage was expanded gradually so that by 1968 it extended to employers of 25 or more. The 1972 amendments lowered this to 15 or more. As is the case with most federal legislation regulating business, employers must be engaged in interstate commerce to be covered by the Act. This requirement has been quite liberally interpreted by the courts over the years so that virtually every business except the small, family-owned restaurant or grocery store is considered to be engaged in interstate commerce. It should be noted, however, that in the public sector the impact of state and local legislation is increasing as personnel and labor relations assume more importance in educational and other public institutions.

One aspect of both state and federal statutes that has a direct effect on the personnel department is that many of the laws require a vast amount of record-keeping to provide information for government inspectors, and some require in addition the filing of periodic reports to various government agencies. Recent legislation has increased the record-keeping requirements so much that smaller firms in particular have had to increase their personnel staffs merely to keep up with the paperwork. Another aspect of government regulation that presents problems for personnel managment is that there are times, especially shortly after the enactment of a federal law, when an employer may be subject to conflicting requirements at the state and federal levels. Sometimes these conflicts are resolved fairly quickly, but there have been times when it has taken several years of litigation in the courts to settle the issues involved.

The history of state and federal legislation in areas affecting personnel management shows a similar pattern over the years. Usually a number of the more progressive and more heavily industrialized states have statutes on the books for a number of years before Congress passes a law setting national standards. Congressional action results from political pressure built up because of those states that have no laws or regulations, or that do not fully enforce the ones that exist. For employers with operations in several states, the advantages of national standards in personnel matters are obvious. For other employers there may be advantages, also. Before the Occupational Safety and Health Act went into effect in 1971, for example, companies in some states could not afford to provide certain safety equipment even though they wanted to. The cost of providing the equipment would have put them at a severe competitive disadvantage. But once all employers involved in the same type of work are required to provide the equipment, the competitive disadvantage disappears.

Legal Influences on Selection—FEP Legislation

Until fairly recently, employers were largely free to select anyone they wanted as an employee, and there was little legal influence in this important area of personnel administration. Fair employment legislation, prohibiting discrimination in employment because of race, sex, age, and certain other factors, has resulted in the selection process itself being subject to legal scrutiny, and the enforcement of these laws at local, state, and federal levels has had a major impact on personnel policies and practices.

New York State enacted the first fair employment practices (FEP) law in 1945, and by the time the federal legislation went into effect, FEP laws were on the books in half the states. But the federal Civil Rights Act of 1964 has provided the greatest impetus to equal opportunity in employment. Title VII of the Act prohibits discrimination in employment based on race, color, religion, national origin, or sex and applies to employers, labor unions, and employment agencies. The enforcement agency for Title VII is the Equal Employment Opportunity Commission (EEOC), and the number of charges of employment discrimination filed with the EEOC grew from 6,000 in 1966 to more than 22,000 in 1971. During this period, however, fewer than half these charges were processed to a settlement because the EEOC had no authority of its own to bring legal action against the employer involved. Amendments passed in 1972 did provide EEOC with the power to bring enforcement actions through the federal courts.

Another program undertaken by the government, which has had a major influence in encouraging equal employment opportunity, applies to companies doing business with the government and their subcontractors. An Executive Order issued in 1970 not only prohibits government contractors from discriminating in employment, but requires further that they take "affirmative action" to eliminate any possibility of discrimination. The enforcement agency for this Order is the Office of Federal Contract Compliance (OFCC) in the U.S. Department of Labor. Investigators throughout the country have authority to look into the personnel practices of the approximately 90,000 establishments subject to OFCC rules for evidence of discrimination and affirmative action.

The initial efforts of both EEOC and OFCC related to charges of racial discrimination, primarily in the hiring process. While all the techniques used in selection have been subjected to investigation for possible discriminatory results, the use of psychological tests has been of greatest concern. The law does stipulate that testing for selection is legal as long as the test is not specifically designed, intended, or used to discriminate. But in a landmark decision handed down in 1971, *Griggs* v. *Duke Power Co.,* the U. S. Supreme Court stated that the crucial issue in the use of tests and other hiring practices is not the employer's intent but the result. Any practice is prohibited if it results in discrimination against a minority group and is not specifically related to actual job performance, according to the court. The significant aspect of this ruling for personnel management is that techniques used for making selection decisions must be proved to be measures of job performance.

In the past two or three years, the government's FEP agencies have moved strongly into the area of sex discrimination. A major difficulty in the enforcement of the ban on sex discrimination is that the law permits such discrimination where sex is a "bona fide occupational qualification," or BFOQ. (The BFOQ exception also applies to discrimination based on religion or nationality but not to racial discrimination.) The interpretation of the BFOQ provision by EEOC has been quite narrow, and many employers have been forced to eliminate formerly all-male or all-female job categories. Another problem arising out of the sex discrimination cases is the conflict with provisions of many state protective laws, which regulate various aspects of working conditions for women such as the maximum weight they can be required to lift. Eventually, EEOC decided that these laws could not be used to deny certain jobs to women, with the result that the protective laws have been repealed or ruled invalid in most states. In addition to the recent concern with sex discrimination, there now is growing concern over the lack of both minorities and women in the higher-paying occupations and in top-level managerial positions. Thus, the whole gamut of personnel policies, including those relating to promotion and to training and development programs, is being reviewed in many firms for possible discriminatory effects.

One other aspect of equal employment opportunity is that of discrimination on the basis of age. This type of discrimination was not covered in the Civil Rights Act, but in 1969 Congress passed the Age Discrimination Act, which includes a BFOQ provision. This law is enforced by the Labor Department rather than the EEOC, and to date there have been relatively few cases brought under it.

Legal Influences on Compensation Policies

Legal influence on compensation policies has a much longer history and a much more direct impact on personnel practices than

is true in the area of selection. In addition to legislation affecting policies on how much an employer may pay his employees, there are a
host of state and federal requirements dictating the procedures for
making payments. These include such matters as how often employees must be paid, whether wages have to be in the form of cash,
whether or how much of an employee's wages are subject to gar-
nishment by creditors, and how much must be withheld for payroll
taxes—income and social security.

The question of how much the company pays and what the rates
should be for different types of work has been influenced by state
and federal minimum wage laws, by direct controls on wage and salary administration during times of economic stress, and since 1963 by
the Equal Pay Act, which prohibits pay differential based on sex. The
Equal Pay Act is related to the civil rights legislation in that its goal is
equal treatment of men and women in employment. The Labor Department generally has been successful in having the courts support
its efforts to enforce the Act by awarding groups of women large
amounts of back pay where it could be shown they were doing essentially the same work as men even though the job titles for the
men were different. As a result, employers have found themselves
reexamining the whole job classification system and pay structure
and making changes in them. A fairly common example is that of
building maintenance, where the "janitors" pay scale has often been
at a higher level than that of the "maids," even though they perform
the same work. Now all come under the same category, "custodial
employees," with the same pay scale.

Mimimum wage legislation goes back to the early 1900s in some
states, and on the national level to 1938 when Congress passed the
Fair Labor Standards Act. The first minimum wage established by the
FLSA was 25 cents an hour; over the years since then amendments to
the law have raised the minimum progressively to the present level
of $1.60 an hour. Most of the states except in the Southeast also have
minimum wage laws, a few of which call for a higher minimum than
the federal law. Both the federal and state laws include provisions requiring payment at premium rates for time worked in excess of a certain number of hours in a specified period of time. The most common standard is the requirement of pay at one and one-half times
the regular rate for work in excess of 40 hours per week. The intent
of the overtime-pay requirement was to limit the length of the workweek indirectly, although a number of states have laws with a speci-

fied limit on the amount of time that can be worked, especially by women and children.

   Direct wage and salary controls result in a number of administrative problems for the personnel manager, but in the instances when they have been imposed they have helped keep wage and salary costs down. Thus, they are viewed by many as a "necessary evil" when the nation's economy is threatened with sharply increased inflation. The most recent "economic emergency" was declared in August 1971 with a 90-day freeze on all general wage and salary increases and nearly all individual pay adjustments. Since then the federal Pay Board has issued various standards and policies on different types of wage and fringe benefit adjustments with a view to keeping increases in wage costs to about 6 percent per year. As in previous periods of federal controls on compensation, the companies with well-established, standardized policies and practices were in the best position to justify granting wage increases needing specific approval.

   A large portion of an employer's compensation cost is for fringe benefits, and these are included in the present government controls program. Many of these benefit programs also are influenced by other state and federal legislation. The monthly payments provided under the federal Social Security Act have an impact on the level of benefits provided under company pension plans, for example. Another large-scale public benefit program is the unemployment compensation (UC) system, which pays weekly sums to employees who lose their jobs through no fault of their own. The existence of the UC system has some bearing on the types of benefits employers might provide for workers subject to layoff. Because it is financed by a tax based on the number of employees the company adds to the ranks of the unemployed, the UC system also influences personnel policy with regard to separations by encouraging the company to keep them at a minimum.

Legal Influences on Working Conditions

   Public concern over the safety of the workplace goes back to the 1800s and the beginnings of industrialization. Many of the state laws restricting hours of work and relating to protection of women and children stemmed from this concern. Prior to 1900, however, there were only a few states with laws setting safety standards and calling for factory inspections. Furthermore, the legal climate during that time protected employers from any costs associated with accidents, partly on the premise that workers accepting jobs also accept the risks involved.

Between 1900 and 1920, the legal climate changed as most of the states enacted workmen's compensation laws providing benefits for employees injured on the job and payments to the families of employees killed in job-related accidents. To keep down the costs of the workmen's compensation insurance, companies now had an incentive to encourage safe practices and procedures. Since that time, safety engineering, employee and supervisory safety training, safety contests, and other safety promotion techniques have been a major aspect of the personnel program in manufacturing industries.

The result of these efforts was that for about 40 years the nation's record in industrial safety showed a slow but steady improvement. During the 1960s, however, a decline set in. This development, along with new problems relating to occupational health and the still-unknown effects of various industrial chemicals and other agents, led to the enactment of the first comprehensive federal legislation in the field. The Occupational Safety and Health Act of 1970 gave the government authority to set and enforce national standards for health and safety on the job, to conduct inspections of the workplace, and to ask the courts to condemn dangerous conditions or practices.

In enforcing the Act, the Labor Department directed its initial efforts primarily at the industries with the worst safety records— longshoring, roofing and sheet metal, meat and meat products, miscellaneous transportation equipment, and lumber and wood products. At the same time, some of the problems of health hazards were subjected to research sponsored by the National Institute for Occupational Safety and Health, which was established by the Act. The results of this research, it is hoped, will provide answers to the many questions remaining in the field of occupational health, and thus offer a valid basis for undertaking new personnel programs in this area.

LABOR RELATIONS

The area within personnel management that is most closely circumscribed by legal considerations is that of labor relations. In companies where employees are represented by unions, a large part of the personnel staff's time and effort is spent on matters relating to dealing with the union. However, the influence of the labor movement extends throughout the economy as nonunionized employers seek to keep pace with union wage levels, often with a conscious view to heading off union organizing attempts. Thus, in union and nonunion firms alike, what happens in labor relations generally has a major influence on personnel decisions.

The Legal Framework

In Chapter 2 we noted that the first federal intervention in the industrial scene on behalf of the unions occurred in the 1930s. Prior to that time, the prevailing attitude in the government and in the court system was that business should be free to operate with a minimum of control over its decisions in labor relations matters. An indication of a change in this attitude came with the passage in 1926 of the Railway Labor Act, which set up procedures for collective bargaining and disputes settlement in the rail transportation industry, one of the most heavily unionized at the time.

For most industries, however, the big change in public policy came with the National Labor Relations Act, or Wagner Act, in 1935. The Wagner Act set forth a list of activities, called unfair labor practices, that were forbidden to management—the first time the government had imposed direct constraints on management actions in relations with unions. The types of actions prohibited by the law included interference with employees' rights to organize and bargain collectively, domination of any labor organization (such as a company union), discharge or other action against any employee filing charges under the act, refusal to bargain collectively with a union duly chosen by employees as their representative, and discrimination because of union membership. Under the latter provision, it was deemed unlawful for employers to use "yellow dog" contracts, to inquire whether job applicants were union members or whether they favored unions, and to fire employees because of union membership—all devices that had been used extensively by management.

The constraints on management provided by the Wagner Act did accomplish the purpose of public support for union efforts, eventually to the point where it was feared that labor had too much power. As a result, in 1947 Congress passed amendments to the Wagner Act known as the Labor Management Relations Act, or the Taft-Hartley Act, commonly referred to as the Taft Act. The Taft Act,

which is based on a concept of the government as the impartial arbi-
ter in union-management affairs, is the basic and most important
federal labor law in operation today. The Taft Act continued the pro-
hibition against unfair labor practices but added provisions guaran-
teeing employers the right to express their views on union representation (the so-called "free speech" amendment), providing
machinery for a representation election to certify a union as bargaining agent (under the Wagner Act such elections were conducted
only when two or more competing unions demanded recognition as
bargaining agent), and giving employers the right to sue unions in
the courts for breach of contract.

While the Wagner and Taft Acts set forth general policy in labor
relations and specified limitations on the activities of both parties, it
is the way the statutes have been interpreted by the NLRB and the
courts that affects personnel decisions. For the personnel administrator, unfortunately, the law has been subject to various inter-
pretations at various times. Not only is there the problem of the
courts often overturning NLRB decisions, and sometimes the process
of judicial review takes years, but there also is the problem of NLRB
itself reversing long-standing precedents. This happens primarily because the NLRB is a political body, whose members are appointed by
the President for a five-year term of office, which tends to change
character with changes in the political party in office. However, the
fact that the Taft Act has remained the basic labor law for more than
25 years probably can be attributed to NLRB's flexibility in reflecting
changes in public sentiment in its decisions.

Because the situation is such that what is lawful today may not
be tomorrow, we will not elaborate on the effects of NLRB rulings in
specific circumstances. Issues that have been raised in a great number of cases include the interpretation of the "free speech" provision, the problem of reinstatement rights of workers who go out on
strike, and what constitutes collective bargaining in "good faith," as
the law requires. Some precedents for handling these issues have
been established over the years, but most cases still are determined
on an individual basis taking into account the facts of the particular
situation. The area of union relations obviously is one where the personnel manager needs all the expert knowledge and advice he can
get.

Another federal law regulating some aspects of union-
management relations is the Landrum-Griffin Act, or the Labor-

Management Reporting and Disclosure Act of 1959. Aimed primarily at regulating internal union affairs to prevent racketeering, the Act does impose some restrictions on managerial activity and requires reports from employers on various types of payments made to unions, to employees, or to labor consultants for the purpose of influencing employees. One purpose of the law was to eliminate *sweetheart contracts,* under which the employer and a union official agree to contract terms that are substandard, to their mutual betterment. The Landrum-Griffin Act also cleared up a problem related to companies engaged in interstate commerce but too small to come within NLRB's jurisdictional standards. Because of the limited funds available, NLRB set certain standards based on volume of business to determine whether it would accept jurisdiction. The result was that some small employers were not covered by either federal or state labor relations statutes. Under Landrum-Griffin the states are given jurisdiction in these situations; however, less than one third of the states have labor relations laws providing the comprehensive protection against abuses on both sides that the Taft Act provides

Within the framework of state and federal laws relating to labor relations, there are alternative approaches available to management in dealing with unions in their organizing efforts, in collective bargaining, and in other aspects of long-term union relations. The presence of a union on the scene adds to the constraints within which the personnel department can operate, and once a collective bargaining agreement is signed the terms of the agreement are factors that have to be taken into account in making personnel decisions. For these reasons, we will discuss the general area of labor relations here rather than in Part II where we describe the various work activities of the personnel department. It should be noted, however, that in unionized companies a large proportion of the work of the personnel or industrial relations staff involves union relations.

Unions and Unionization

As indicated in the previous discussion, the union situation may be completely different from one company to another or even from one division of the same company to another. It can range from one where management and the union have a well-established bargaining relationship extending back over some 30 years or more to one where there is no union in the picture at all and not likely to be one. In between, there are situations where the parties have a newly established bargaining relationship and considerable testing of each other's power occurs or situations where management is heavily engaged in activities designed to keep a union from being successful in an organizing attempt. The latter strategy seems to have been particularly effective in the period since the mid-1950s. In 1956 union membership in the United States was 17.5 million, which represented 25.2 percent of the total labor force; by 1963 it had declined to 16.5 million. By 1968 it had grown to 18.9 million, but this was only 23 percent of the labor force.

The growth in overall union membership gives some indication of the power of labor on a national scale, but there are a number of other factors related to a union's power on the local level. These include whether it is a craft or an industrial union, whether it is an independent or part of a national or international union, and whether it is affiliated with the AFL-CIO. Another factor contributing to the union's power is whether it represents a large share or only a small segment of the company's employees. A union that represents all the production, maintenance, and office workers normally has considerable power, although on occasion a relatively small group, if in a strategic position, also may have an inordinate amount of power. Important considerations in assessing union strength are how secure the leader's position is and the nature of the community environment. Unions generally can be expected to be more successful in industrialized areas in the Northeast and Great Lakes regions which are considered "union towns" than in the far less unionized Southeast. In former years, the type of worker was a major factor in unionization. Recent gains in union membership, however, have been greatest among teachers, retail clerks, and government workers, all of which are considered white-collar occupations and include large numbers of women. Both groups were viewed as generally antiunion in the past.

All these factors should be taken into account in assessing a union's potential for confrontation, whether the situation involves an organizing attempt or collective bargaining strategy. No matter how strong the union appears to be in an organizing situation, however management's actions almost always are geared to keeping the union out. It is generally conceded that employees who are dissatisfied with some aspect of their working conditions are the ones most susceptible to union appeals. Therefore, any steps management can take to keep employees satisfied tend to help head off the union. However, such policies have to be undertaken on a long-term basis to be effective. Once a union has actually made progress in signing up employees, any obvious steps taken by management may be viewed as an attempt to "buy" employee support with no guarantee that should the union in fact be discouraged the company would not go back to its old ways.

When a union has been able to sign up 30 percent or more of the employee group it wants to represent, it can petition the NLRB for a representation election. At this point management has to be extremely careful that nothing it does can be construed as interference with the election and thus an unfair labor practice. This probably is one of the most difficult situations a company, and its personnel department in particular, can face. Besides getting expert advice from its own legal staff or outside consultants, management needs to keep all its ranks from first-level supervisor up informed as to what they can and cannot do or say during the organizing campaign. It may be very difficult to keep things on an even keel, especially when management feels that the employees are being ungrateful or disloyal if they vote for the union. The personnel manager, especially, may become very defensive if he views a possible union victory as an indication of his own personal failure. However, everything possible should be done to avoid open conflicts and feelings of bitterness. Aside from the possibility of unfair-labor-practice charges should the union lose the election, if the union should win and thus be certified as bargaining agent, the company is in a far better position at the bargaining table when its prior actions have done nothing to contribute to a hostile environment.

Collective Bargaining

Under the law, once a union has been certified as bargaining agent for a group of employees, management is required to bargain with the union and to do so in "good faith." From this point on, the company's personnel or labor relations staff will devote major effort to negotiating with the union on the terms of a collective bargaining agreement, to handling disputes over the interpretation of the agreement, and to preparing for the next round of negotiations to amend the agreement. The agreement itself becomes a direct influence on personnel decision; in many matters it will limit the courses of action management can take.

The in's and out's of the bargaining process can be extremely complex and are dependent on such variables as the power of the union, management's assessment of this power, and the type of bargaining relationship built up in the past. This relationship may be characterized as one of open conflict, containment, accommodation, or cooperation. Usually the management bargaining committee has authority to negotiate a final settlement, but the union bargaining committee does not. The final agreement must be ratified by a vote of the membership before it can become effective, and proposed settlements often have been rejected where the union negotiators presumably were not attuned to the desires of the members.

The basic issue in most collective bargaining is wages and/or benefits, with the union traditionally asking for "more." Within an industry, the monetary settlements tend to be similar. Often the union concentrates its efforts on negotiating a settlement with a leading firm in the industry with the expectation that the other firms in the same industry will accept the same settlement rather than risk a strike and loss of market. In addition to this type of *pattern bargaining,* some industries are characterized by *coordinated bargaining* in which either the leading firms bargain together as a single unit with one union, or several unions representing different units of a company bargain together, on major issues. Coordinated bargaining results in separate contracts with some common provisions. *Coalition bargaining* involves two or more unions bargaining with one company for a common master agreement covering all employees represented by the unions. The two terms, however, often are used interchangeably.

To initiate the bargaining process, the union submits a list of demands for wage increases and contract provisions that have been voted on by the membership. Management may come to the bargaining table with an offer prepared on the basis of information from wage surveys and other sources, or it may wait to see what the union asks for before presenting an offer. The negotiating process leads to a settlement that will fall somewhere between the union's demands and the company's offer. Under an approach called *Boulwarism* (after Lemuel R. Boulware, former vice president of General Electric Company), the company presented its offer on what the union regarded as a "take it or leave it" basis and refused to change the terms of the initial proposal because of strike threats or to accommodate union political needs. As practiced by GE in one series of negotiations, however, the approach was found to be unlawful under the Taft Act as not bargaining in good faith.

In instances where the parties appear to have irreconcilable differences, conflict, in the form of a strike, may be avoided by calling in a third party to facilitate reaching a settlement. This intervention usually involves *mediation* or *conciliation* by a government representative provided by the Federal Mediation and Conciliation Service. Established by the Taft Act, the FMCS must be notified of any situation in which the parties have not reached agreement on a new contract 30 days prior to the expiration date of the old contract. Mediators have no power to force settlements on the parties, but they often have been successful in helping the parties come to agreement. Another process, that of *arbitration,* involves submitting the issues in dispute to an outside individual or board whose decision then is binding on both parties. Arbitration is rarely used in the bargaining situation except in areas of public interest, such as hospitals and police protection, where the unions represent employees of government agencies. The national-emergency-disputes provisions of the Taft Act call for further intervention by the President if a threatened strike would "imperil the national health or safety." Thus, there are a number of ways the parties are encouraged to reach an agreement without the union's having to resort to a strike, and in fact the vast majority of contract negotiations are concluded without strike action.

The Bargaining Agreement—The end result of the negotiating process is the collective bargaining agreement, a legal contract. Most contracts now run for three years with provision either for additional wage increases in the second and third years or reopening of negotiations on wages only at some point during the contract term. The major provisions of the contract set forth the policies and practices to be followed with regard to all employees in the bargaining unit in such matters as wages and hours of work, disciplinary procedures, employee benefits and services, promotion, transfer, layoff, job security, and seniority. Most contracts also contain a no-strike clause and provide some machinery for the settlement of disputes during the term of the agreement.

A contract provision of major concern to management is the *management rights* clause, which may be in the form of a general statement or a detailed list of specific areas in which the employer retains his freedom to act. In some cases, management prefers not to include any such provision in the contract on the theory that it has these rights anyway and any mention of them might actually be restrictive. With or without such a clause, the current view, as expressed by arbitrators and judges, is that management has an obligation to notify and discuss with the union any action affecting the employees represented by the union. Particularly in situations involving plant relocation or shutdown, the rights that employees have built up over the years with the company must be taken into account.

The contract provision of primary concern to the union is the one relating to union security, which sets forth the union membership requirements of the workers in the bargaining unit. Even though management generally does not like union security agreements because they force employees to join or pay dues to the union whether they want to or not, more than nine out of 10 contracts have some form of provision for union security, except where such provisions are forbidden by state *right-to-work laws.* These laws are found in 19 states, mostly in the South and Great Plains regions.

The most common forms of union security are the following:

> *Union Shop,* which requires all employees in the bargaining unit to become members of the union and maintain their membership throughout the life of the agreement. Under a *modified union shop,* the provision applies only to specified employees, usually those hired after the effective date of the agreement.

> *Maintenance of membership,* which requires that all employees who join the union maintain their membership throughout the contract term but does not require any one to join the union as a condition of employment.

> *Agency shop,* which requires that employees who choose not to join the union nevertheless pay the union the equivalent of union dues. Some right-to-work laws permit this type of union security provision.

Two types of union security that were prohibited by the Taft Act are the *closed shop,* under which only union members can be hired, and the *preferential shop,* under which union members are given preference in hiring. Another aspect of union security is the *check-off* provision, which calls for the company to deduct union dues from the wages of all union members authorizing such a procedure.

Other contract provisions of special interest to the union are those that outline the privileges and responsibilities of the union representatives, particularly the union steward in each designated work group. It is the steward's responsibility to see to it that the agreement is followed and to help with employee complaints over matters covered by the contract.

Grievances and Arbitration—From an employee relations point of view, the heart of the collective bargaining agreement is the machinery for handling grievances. It is because most nonunion firms do not have any formal, impartial procedures for handling employee complaints that union representation often is appealing to the work force. While the grievance procedure may be used as a method of interpreting the contract where its meaning or intent is not clear, most grievances involve employee disciplinary problems. Presumably these same types of problems exist in nonunion companies also, and a few companies have established formal grievance procedures for nonunionized groups of employees.

The typical grievance procedure specifies a series of steps beginning with the employee or the union steward, or both, discussing the complaint with the immediate supervisor; the complaint then goes through successively higher levels of both management and union officials. If the issue is not resolved by the final step of the procedure, it goes to arbitration for settlement by an impartial umpire chosen by mutual consent of the parties or appointed by the FMCS or the American Arbitration Association (AAA). While nearly all union contracts call for arbitration as the final recourse for resolving grievances, the procedures in nonunionized firms rarely do.

Because the operation of the grievance machinery is such an important aspect of day-to-day employee relations, most companies go to a great deal of effort to see that it is effective. Special programs are undertaken to keep supervisors informed as to employee rights under the contract and of any changes made in the provisions of the agreement. Some companies even provide special training in handling grievances for both union stewards and supervisors. The goal of these programs is to keep the number of grievances to a minimum, and particularly to keep as few as possible from going to arbitration, which is a very costly procedure. However, management might well be suspicious if there is a complete lack of grievances in a particular department. Such a situation may indicate that the supervisors are not doing anything about employee violations of the contract; this in turn could cause even bigger problems in the future.

Union Tactics

Despite management's best efforts to avoid open conflict situations, strikes and other union-related work stoppages do occur. In the early stages of union activity, strikes are most likely to be over issues of union recognition and jurisdiction; as the union relationship matures, strike issues tend to revolve around wages and working conditions, fringe benefits, and job security.

The majority of strikes are economic in nature because the action is taken to back union demands for increased wages or benefits or for changes in the collective bargaining agreement that will be of benefit to the workers covered by the agreement. Other types of strikes that occur less frequently but nevertheless pose difficulties for management include (1) *unfair-labor-practices strikes,* in which workers protest against an alleged unfair labor practice on the part of management; (2) *jurisdictional strikes,* in which two or more unions try to force recognition as bargaining agent; and (3) *sympathy strikes,* in which a union with no dispute of its own with an employer uses a strike to register support for the demands of another union. The most common tactic used in these kinds of strikes is *picketing,* although sometimes picketing may be carried on without any strike activity. This is done frequently when the issue is union recognition; in this case it is called *organizational picketing.* Another type of picketing is aimed at forcing companies with which the union has no dispute not to use products of an employer with whom it does have a dispute. This is called a *secondary boycott,* and such tactics are now illegal in situations covered by the Taft Act.

One type of concerted strike activity that can cause a good deal of disruption is the *wildcat strike,* a strike that has not been authorized by the membership or higher union authority. A lesser version of the wildcat strike is a *slowdown,* in which the workers interfere with normal production processes in a variety of ways. Both these tactics often are used to protest management actions during the term of the contract when a no-strike clause prohibits concerted action in support of the union, or employee, position in a dispute.

Strikes stemming from contract negotiations usually come as no surprise to management. The union has to have a vote of the membership to call a strike and sets a deadline for the strike to occur if there is no agreement on a new contract. As the deadline approaches, management must make a deliberate decision as to whether it should give in to the union's demands or accept the strike. If the demands are such that the company would lose more by giving in than by taking the strike, then management has to be prepared with a course of action. In a situation where the union is strong with large financial resources, a long strike can be anticipated and management should make its plans accordingly. In the past, a strike by any large group of workers usually resulted in a complete shutdown; increasingly, however, companies are deciding to continue operations during a strike. In industries with automated production operations, supervisors and other managerial employees can keep production at near normal levels for a considerable time.

Because of the decreased effectiveness of the strike in many industries and also because of the complexities involved in technological changes affecting unionized employees, a number of employers and unions have experimented with some different approaches to bargaining. These attempts at "creative collective bargaining" usually involve provision for continuous contact between the parties, and possibly also for a third party representing the public to discuss and try to resolve the issues in dispute. When these programs were adopted in the early 1960s there were high hopes that they might point the way to labor peace, but to date this has not been the case. Strikes, slowdowns, and picketing remain the ultimate weapons in the union arsenal, and the threat of such activity remains a major influence on personnel management decisions.

OTHER INFLUENCES

The primarily legal environment discussed so far in this chapter often dictates answers to questions of what can and what cannot be done in making personnel decisions. In addition, there are factors that point to the most effective of several possible approaches to a particular personnel matter. These factors include the results of personnel research, conducted either by staff units within the organization or by outside consultants, and the organizational climate as reflected in the top-management value system.

Personnel Research

For many years much of the research in personnel management consisted of surveys dealing with the frequency with which companies followed certain practices. Although the survey reports usually broke down the results by categories such as company size or type of industry, there was little indication of why certain practices were more common than others or whether a particular type of program was considered successful in contributing to good employee relations. Thus, a personnel staffer assigned the task of making recommendations for an employee sick-leave policy, for example, might have nothing more to go on than a survey report indicating that about half the firms in the same industry provided such a benefit.

Recently this situation has improved considerably. Not only are much more detailed statistics available providing breakdowns by occupations involved, local practices, and so forth, but also reports of controlled experiments indicating measures of effectiveness of various personnel techniques and programs are becoming available. In Chapter 2, we noted the tremendous increase in personnel research activities over the past 20 to 30 years in both the academic and business worlds. Despite this growth, personnel research staffs of any size still seem to be limited to the nation's largest corporations, with A.T.&T., Standard Oil of New Jersey, IBM, Xerox, GE, Sears, Roebuck, and J. C. Penney being outstanding examples.

A major emphasis in the research of these staffs is testing the validity of a particular technique through experimental studies. This is accomplished by using the technique with one group of employees but not with another, and then measuring any differences in subsequent job behavior. In Part II we will go into more detail on some of the problems inherent in this type of research, such as what criterion is most appropriate for determining superior job performance. However, one requirement for experimental research which is of concern at this point is that it be repeated. In other words, the results of an initial study need to be replicated with a second group of employees to be considered generally applicable. Often the initial results do not hold up on repetition, particularly if the replication study involves employees of a different company, in different jobs, or at different locations within the same firm.

What has become increasingly clear from recent personnel research efforts is that techniques or programs that work with one group of employees may not be at all effective with another group.

While it can be hoped that generalizable solutions to personnel problems may evolve in the future, the state of the art at the moment is that even solutions that were thought to be valid across organizations probably are not. This presents real difficulties for the personnel administrator in an organization that cannot afford a large personnel research staff. Increasingly, outside consultants are being called upon to undertake research studies as a guide to formulating personnel policy.

The Use of Consultants

The use of outside experts or consultants for advice in personnel matters is a longstanding and widespread practice. A 1971 BNA survey showed that nearly three out of four companies had called in one or more consultants to help solve personnel problems during the previous five years; one company had used 20 different consultants during that period. The area in which outside expertise was most frequently sought is that of compensation—the setting up of job evaluation and wage administration procedures and the planning of pension and other employee benefit programs. There are several large consulting firms that specialize in compensation matters for hundreds of companies throughout the nation. Consultants also work on an individual basis, and many university professors perform personnel consulting services on a part-time basis.

For small and medium-sized companies, the use of outside consultants on personnel matters has major advantages. In terms of cost, the company gets the benefit of expert knowledge without adding permanently to the payroll. Also, the consultant can focus all his efforts on the problem at hand; he does not have to be concerned about his position in the organization or his relationship with subordinates; he can point out previous errors or policy deficiencies. Perhaps the biggest difficulty in the use of personnel consultants is that programs and policies they recommend on the basis of their studies are not always implemented. Often a company is willing to pay a consultant to make a study and suggest a course of action but unwilling to put the action into effect. The basic problem here usually is the unwillingness or the inability of the personnel executive to convince top management of the efficacy of the consultant's proposed program. This situation is very likely to occur if the proposal involves considerable long-term expense and the benefits are not apparent or if the changes required to implement the proposal go against the traditional values of the business establishment.

Organizational Climate

This brings us to the influence on personnel decisions of the organizational climate or management value system. Nearly every article in the personnel literature that provides pointers on how to undertake a particular program either begins or ends with the admonition, "The interest and support of higher management are *essential* for the success of this program!" While this may be an obvious truism, it often is neglected in the planning of personnel programs.

Sometimes the top-management influence is obvious, as in an example reported by a personnel executive responding to a BNA survey on older workers. He explained that no matter how much money might be saved, a policy requiring compulsory retirement at any age would not be adopted in his firm because "the company founder and chief executive officer is in his 80s and still going strong." Often, however, certain values of the chief executive may not be so easy to ascertain; in fact he may not even be aware of opinions and feelings himself. Some of the newer executive development programs are aimed at uncovering these unconscious influences that may be blocking administrative effectiveness.

One of the personnel manager's tasks, then, is to evaluate the managerial climate of his organization and to take this into account in deciding what policies to recommend. He may well recommend an effort to change whatever climate he finds, if the top executive supports such a program. However, if the personnel executive finds the climate antithetical to his own value system and there is very little likelihood of changing it, he can anticipate a good deal of frustrations and conflict.

In the past, personnel people, especially those imbued with the human relations philosophy, often have experienced frustration and conflicts. The programs they proposed to increase worker satisfaction rarely were related to dollars-and-cents benefits; top management might go along or experiment with such programs when profits were high, but they were quickly abandoned when times were bad. As certain behavioral scientists increasingly turn their attention to questions of employee motivation and productivity and overall organizational effectiveness, it can be expected that future innovations in personnel policies and practices will be more closely related to productivity goals, and thus more likely to be compatible with top-management values.

In Part I we have tried to present a framework covering the historical, legal, and other influences that may affect the operation of personnel management today. In Part II we will discuss the major activities that fall within the personnel bailiwick, and where appropriate indicate the impact of these influences on a particular activity. A major concern will be the results of scientific research in those areas where such research has been reported.

PART II

The Personnel Process

CHAPTER 4

Personnel Planning

We turn now to the personnel process—the activities carried on by the personnel department in its role of formulating and implementing policy with respect to the organization's human resources. The first set of activities to be considered are those of a planning nature; in one sense the results of these activities serve to set the stage for other personnel activities. Thus, organization planning determines the number and types of managerial positions to be staffed now, and manpower planning provides an indication of the numbers and types of employees who will be needed at some point in the future. Other aspects of personnel planning to be discussed in this chapter include employee information systems, which provide the data needed for effective planning, and job analysis, which defines personnel requirements throughout the lower levels of the organization. Taken together, these activities provide an indication of the mix of people and skills required to carry on the work necessary to achieve the organization's goals. In essence, they define what the personnel department should be doing in the areas of recruiting, selection, and training to keep the organization operating effectively in the future.

ORGANIZATION PLANNING

Organization planning focuses on the company structure with the objective of developing the type of structure that will be most effective in achieving organizational goals. The planning process begins with the top of the organization, and the jurisdictions of those reporting to the chief executive officer predetermine the overall structure. In a firm organized on a functional basis, for example, there will be vice presidents of manufacturing, of marketing, and of finance reporting to the president. If a regional structure is used, there will be titles such as vice president-western region, vice president-central region, and vice president-eastern region. Another type of structure is based on the different products or services a firm provides, as in a bank with separate vice presidents in charge of checking accounts, savings accounts, loans, and trusts.

As the planning process continues down through the management hierarchy, the end result is an organization chart with a slot for every position, indicating who reports to whom and providing some idea of the scope of the position in terms of authority and responsibility. The chart sometimes is accompanied by position descriptions and/or policy manuals with more detail. While there is no ideal structure for all organizations, because of the many different types of task objectives, there are certain characteristics that seem to contribute to effectiveness. These include such things as making sure there are no areas of overlapping jurisdiction and providing clear and unambiguous statements of each manager's role. Another important consideration that sometimes is neglected relates to the personalities and capabilities of the people actually in the positions. A finance vice president who is a topnotch analyst but uncomfortable working with people would be more effective in his job with an assistant vice president to supervise the department heads in his jurisdiction.

The Planning Group

While all organizations have a structure, whether it is depicted graphically in chart form or not, relatively few have a separate group for organization planning, and many such units that do exist are relatively new. By and large, changes in organization structure do not come about through formal planning efforts but evolve as a result of decisions made at top-management levels. These are decisions relating to such matters as entering a new market, manufacturing a new product, or merging with another company. After such a decision is made, the board of directors or the chief executive then determines what changes are needed in the organization structure to carry out the decision.

Where organization planning units do exist, they carry on continuing studies with a view to developing an ideal future plan for maximum goal achievement. In some instances, they even have authority to determine who is to be assigned the top positions. Typically, these planning units are not in the exclusive jurisdiction of the personnel department; they may report directly to the chief executive officer rather than to the top personnel executive, although the personnel department may be represented in the unit.

Variables in Organization Structures

The planning group needs to take into account a number of variables in developing an ideal structure. These include matters relating to decision making—whether such authority should be centralized at the top or decentralized in the various divisions; division of labor—the number of departments there should be and whether the work of each department should be defined narrowly or cover a range of activities; and the length of the chain of command—how many levels of management there should be from the lowest rank-and-file worker to the chief executive. The way all these questions are answered has implications for the personnel department in that the answers serve to specify the positions that must be staffed.

One variable that is of particular interest to the personnel manager and that has generated a good deal of research is the span of control, or the number of individuals reporting to a single manager. This is related to the chain of command, in that the larger the number of individuals reporting to each manager, the fewer the levels of management, or the flatter the organization structure. In tall organizations, with many levels between the worker and the top executive, there will be a smaller number of employees reporting to each manager. No matter how desirable it may be to reduce the number of management levels for one reason or another, the research on span of control indicates that there is a point at which organizational effectiveness is adversely affected by increasing the number of employees supervised by a single manager.

While the optimal span for most situations appears to be in the range of 5 to 10 employees per manager, there are a number of factors to be taken into account such as the type of work being performed, the amount of control required, and the previous experience of both employees and supervisor. From the personnel viewpoint, the important thing to recognize is that as a manager's workload increases it may not be possible to add more and more new employees to handle the work and obtain the same level of performance. There is likely to come a point where a change in structure—a new department or a different division of labor—is needed.

MANPOWER PLANNING

Some aspects of manpower planning, such as the use of management inventories to indicate training needs, date back to World War II and the work of the War Manpower Commission. As in the case of organization planning, however, the concept of formal manpower planning as a major personnel activity is fairly recent and is still not widespread, except in large organizations. While organization planning deals with the existing and future *structure* of the firm, manpower planning has the objective of ensuring that the *people* needed to staff the structure will be available. The results of organization planning, especially if they are stated in the form of an ideal future structure, constitute one of the variables to be taken into account in manpower planning. If a company decides to move in the direction of a flatter organization with fewer management levels, for example, there may be a smaller number of management positions to fill in the future than there are now. If the same company anticipates considerable growth, however, additional managers may be needed in spite of the change in organization structure. Both these factors are included in manpower forecasting, the first step in manpower planning.

Forecasting Future Manpower Needs

Some type of forecasting of future manpower needs is conducted by nearly all companies. In many instances, such forecasting is limited to the short term and involves such procedures as asking department heads to submit reports on job vacancies and estimates of anticipated losses from turnover and retirement for the next few months or a year. Somewhat longer range forecasts may be undertaken with reference to a specific known development. This occurs, for example, if a new department is to be added or a new plant built and it is necessary to determine what personnel will be required to staff the new operation.

Long-range forecasting attempts to predict needs for various types of manpower at a point in time as much as five to 10 years in the future This procedure involves the use of a predictor, such as sales volume, that is known to have a historical relationship with manpower requirements. Forecasts of future sales then are used to indicate future manpower needs. Different predictor variables may be necessary for different types of manpower, and the resulting estimate may need to be adjusted in the light of long-range plans for expansion or for changes in the organization structure.

Determining Future Manpower Supplies

Whether manpower planning is done on a long- or short-term basis, the second step is to determine the existing manpower resources within the company. This can be accomplished by estimating the number of positions that will become vacant over the forecasting period and indicating the employees who now are available to fill the positions. Sometimes a chart is prepared for each department listing each managerial job with a projection of how long the incumbent is likely to remain, and a list of possible candidates to replace him is appended.

A summary of these inventory charts together with information from estimates of promotions, demotions, and transfers, based on past experience, provides a picture of the internal manpower supply. Another component of the supply side is an estimate of the number and kinds of new employees that will be added, assuming that hiring is continued at the present rate.

The Manpower Projection

The estimated manpower supply is then compared with the forecast of manpower needs. The result of this comparison is the essence of manpower planning for personnel management. If it appears that manpower supply and demand will be in balance, little change is required in the organization's employment policies. If supply is likely to exceed demand in the future, recruiting and hiring activities may need to be curtailed for a period of time, and employees may have to be laid off or transferred to other operations.

Where the projection indicates that manpower needs will be much in excess of supply, a number of approaches may be indicated depending on how many and what types of new employees will be needed. Increased recruiting is an obvious solution in many instances, but this may not be sufficient in all situations. By using data on projections of the national labor force, available from the government, it is possible to determine future skill shortages that are likely to occur throughout the country. Where there are such anticipated national shortages, employers may undertake programs to train employees in new skills or provide support for university or other programs of an educational nature. Approaches other than training include redesigning jobs so that certain skills are not required for as many jobs as before and raising compensation levels to attract people with the needed skills or experience.

In recent years, manpower planning has been a favorite subject in the personnel literature, mostly as a result of experience in the late 1950s and 1960s with shortages of various technical and scientific manpower. Relatively few companies, however, engage in the type of long-range manpower planning that has been advocated by many writers in the field. Because of the time and expense involved in making long-range forecasts and adjusting them on a periodic basis, it is usually only the largest firms that do undertake such programs. For the small employer, hiring only a few individuals in any one skill category each year, the cost of a comprehensive manpower planning effort would not be worth the benefits realized. Such efforts are of value, nevertheless, when a company is planning a major expansion, or if past experience indicates that there may be a need to hire large numbers of people with certain skills at some future date.

Long-range manpower forecasting at the national level is extremely valuable if as a result educational programs geared to alleviating projected skill shortages are instituted and expanded. Such programs help large and small employers alike by assuring adequate manpower supplies.

EMPLOYEE INFORMATION SYSTEMS

Some type of employee information system is essential for every personnel operation no matter how large or how small. Certain data on each employee—name, social security number, wages paid—are required for payroll-tax purposes, and other information often is needed for governmental record-keeping requirements. Increasingly, systems for maintaining and processing employee information are being computerized.

With a computerized system it is possible to obtain much of the data needed for both organization and manpower planning relatively easily. Most companies, however, have not extended the use of the computer for employee information purposes much beyond the basic personal data needed on each employee and payroll processing. An approach that is being used in an increasing number of organizations is a personnel, or skills, inventory. Such an inventory is possible in very small firms without the aid of a computer, but for most companies a computer is a basic requirement.

Personnel Inventories

The details included in a personnel inventory information system vary from one company to another, but the data generally are of two kinds—

1. Employee skills, including education and training programs completed, prior experience, specialized skills such as knowledge of foreign languages, and aptitude- and/or personality-test scores.

2. Performance data, indicating how the employee is performing on his present job, what weaknesses he has if any, what type of training he needs if any, and his potential for promotion to a higher level job.

Data in the first category are obtained from application blanks and questionnaires filled out by the employee or his supervisor; one or more of the employee's superiors supplies the performance data. Another input sometimes included in the system is that of employee preference; employees may be asked outright if they are interested in advancement and into what types of jobs, or supervisors may be asked to find this out informally. When the personnel inventory data are processed, the result is a picture of the present and potential capabilities of the work force. With some knowledge of future manpower needs, the personnel inventory can be used to indicate areas where more recruiting or training is called for.

A primary reason for setting up a computerized employee information system of this kind is to facilitate a promotion-from-within policy. In large organizations, in particular, it is difficult for a supervisor with a job vacancy to know if there are employees already on the payroll who might qualify. With the personnel inventory stored in a computer, it is a matter of minutes before a list of all qualified (and interested) employees is available.

To date experience with computerized employee information systems has not been entirely positive, and some companies have discontinued them or stopped updating their skills inventories. One problem has been that the computer programs often have been set up to include much information that is not used. With more experience as to the specific items that are useful, this problem may be overcome. In a number of instances, however, it has been found that the personnel inventory simply is not used, sometimes because of resistance to the idea of centralized, computerized decision-making in the realm of employee relations. Overcoming this type of resistance may require considerable long-term management training, and there is some evidence that this training may not be worth the effort. Except in labor-intensive nonmanufacturing companies, such as financial institutions, and very large manufacturing units, it appears that a noncomputerized personnel filing system, combined with managerial knowledge of the work force, can accomplish just as much as a complex computerized operation, at far less cost.

JOB ANALYSIS

Whether an employee information system is computerized or not, the data included have to be related to the requirements of the jobs or positions to be filled if they are to make a maximum contribution to the management of the organizations's human resources. This information relating to job requirements results from the process of job analysis. Job analysis provides a detailed picture of the job structure of the organization—a description of each type of job and the interrelationships between jobs. In most companies, job analysis is carried out only with respect to jobs up to a certain level, and includes only those positions where a detailed statement of the tasks, duties, and responsibilities of the job is desirable. Higher level positions, which are defined primarily in terms of overall responsibilities rather than specific tasks, are incorporated in organization planning and the resultant organization structure.

The technical difference between a job and a position is an important one in discussing job analysis. A *position* is a specific set of tasks and duties performed by an individual employee; a company has as many positions as there are employees. A *job* usually involves a number of the same or similar positions. Thus all employees in positions of bank teller, for example, are considered to have the same job. At the lower levels of the company, the positions are grouped together and studied on the basis of a *job analysis*; at higher levels, where only one individual performs certain tasks, the term *position analysis* may be used.

The information provided by a job or position analysis is basic to the personnel function. It is essential for effective selection procedures: How can people be hired without knowledge of the jobs to be filled? It establishes criteria for evaluating employee performance: How can a supervisor tell if an employee is doing well without a statement as to what behavior the job requires? Job analysis data also are used in job evaluation programs for wage and salary administration purposes, to help determine training needs, and to identify jobs with safety hazards, as well as in other aspects of employee relations.

Job Analysis Techniques

The technique or method used to study a particular job depends on a number of factors—the nature of the job itself, the personnel available to perform the job analysis, and whether an initial effort is involved or an attempt to update a previous analysis. In the latter case, the job description resulting from the earlier analysis serves as a starting point. Job analysts often rely on other job descriptions as a basis for studies of jobs within their own organizations. One frequently used source is the *Dictionary of Occupational Titles* (DOT), which is available from the U.S. Employment Service (USES) and includes brief descriptions of more than 20,000 jobs.

Techniques commonly used in job analysis, in addition to examining existing job descriptions, include observing a number of current job occupants and writing a narrative description, or noting items on a job-description checklist; interviewing job occupants to elicit the necessary information; asking the job occupants themselves to write a description or fill out a job-checklist questionnaire; examining work materials used in performance of the job; or actually performing the job. Each of these techniques has certain advantages and disadvantages which make them more or less appropriate for different types of jobs. Observation of job occupants will not provide much information where the work is largely mental in nature and is too time-consuming when the job cycle, the time from the beginning to the end of a specific task, extends over a long period of time. Actual performance of the work activities of the job also is too time-consuming for many jobs, but this method has been used in connection with such jobs as retail clerk and truck driver. Interviewing and descriptions by job occupants both may be subject to distortion, although some recent research on job analysis indicates that descriptions provided by job occupants are surprisingly accurate and quite consistent.

Whatever the method used, the end product of the job study is a written description containing all the items that have been determined to be relevant. The items included depend both on the nature of the job and on the purposes for which the analysis is to be used. If the purpose is to set up a job evaluation system, the data may cover somewhat different items than if the analysis is to be used solely for hiring.

Certain types of data are found in most job descriptions, however. These include the following:

1. *Job Title*—a name and/or number or code used for bookkeeping purposes.

2. *Work Activities*—specific tasks performed, materials or machines used, interactions with other workers required, nature of supervision necessary, and supervisory duties performed as part of the job.

3. *Conditions of Employment*—the level of the job and its position in the job structure, hours of work, method of payment and fringe benefits payable, and whether the job is full- or part-time and permanent or temporary.

4. *Work Environment*—physical aspects, such as location and the presence of any hazardous or unpleasant condition, and social aspects, such as the number and characteristics of others in the work group.

5. *Job Specification*—the characteristics such as education, experience, skills, and other personal qualifications necessary for the performance of the job. Items listed in the job specification should be related to actual work performance and thus cannot be determined through job analysis alone. It has been found, for example, that a high school diploma is listed as a requirement for many jobs which do not require so much education. Wherever possible, the items listed in the job specification should be based on studies using performance evaluation, which will be discussed in Chapter 5.

Job Families and Career Ladders

Information from job analysis is used initially to indicate what jobs have to be performed in each department or work unit of the organization and how the jobs relate to each other in terms of work assignments. Another relationship that can be derived from job analysis is the degree of similarity among jobs, in terms of the tasks

required or of the personal aptitudes or other characteristics necessary, even among jobs which have different names and appear in
widely separated departments. This grouping of jobs into job families
is extremely helpful to the personnel administrator in matters of employee placement, transfer, and promotion.

One way of grouping jobs is on the basis of requirements for different degrees of aptitudes such as intelligence, verbal or numerical
ability, manual dexterity, and the like. Thus, all the jobs in the company that require a high degree of intelligence and little manual dexterity would be included in the same job family. People presumably
would be able to transfer from one job to another within the job
family more successfully than they could move across families. In this
type of grouping, the job families are established primarily on a horizontal basis with one family for all low-level, unskilled jobs; several
intermediate families of clerical or manual jobs; and the highest
level family encompassing supervisory and other jobs requiring the
highest intelligence and verbal ability. This method of establishing
job families does facilitate movement from one work group to another, but it does little to encourage upward movement within the
company.

Another approach, which appears to be gaining favor, is that of
the career ladder in which jobs are grouped vertically on the basis of
similar skill requirements but with varying levels. Each job in the
same family at a higher level incorporates all the work activities of
the jobs at lower levels; the assumption is that with a certain amount
of actual work experience, and some extra training or outside education, an employee can be upgraded to higher level jobs in the same
career ladder. A major benefit of this approach is the elimination of
dead-end jobs at the lower levels.

Job Design

One criticism of job analysis, and a reason for the development
of career ladders, is that the analysis process results in too rigid a job
structure with little or no room for individual development. On the
premise that employees will be motivated to better work performance if jobs are less restrictive, new approaches to job design have
been introduced in some companies.

One of these concepts is that of job enlargement, or job enrichment. The emphasis in these programs is on incorporating many dif-

ferent tasks in the same job, thus enlarging the scope of one employee's job to include tasks formerly performed by others. When this enlargement on a horizontal basis is accompanied by increased discretion or decision-making so that the employee takes on some duties of his superior, it is called job enrichment. A common example is where workers are given responsibility for the inspection of their own production.

Another increasingly popular approach is that of management by objectives (MBO). While MBO is used primarily as a tool for performance appraisal and individual development, its application results in establishing prescriptions for what a job incumbent should accomplish over a specified period of time. Often the tasks to be performed in achieving the desired goals, which would be clearly specified under job analysis, are not mentioned at all. It is up to the individual employee to decide how he will meet his objectives; in effect, he determines his own job description.

Both these methods of job design—job enlargement and MBO—have been quite successful in certain situations, but it is clear that they are more effective with some types of employees than with others. Workers with little desire for independence and personal growth, for example, do not appear to respond favorably to either program. Even where programs such as MBO are being undertaken, some aspects of job analysis are necessary to provide overall coordination of the job structure to get the work done.

It is likely that in many firms, job analysis has been used in such a way that it has built rigidity into the personnel system; it may be that jobs should be structured as much as possible with the individual's capabilities and interests in mind. The move toward position analysis which takes into account the particular job incumbent reflects this approach. But this is not feasible where very large numbers of workers performing the same job are involved. Such an approach is found primarily in the process of organization planning at higher levels.

Information from the various personnel planning activities discussed in this chapter—organization planning, manpower planning, employee information systems, and job analysis—is used to determine the kinds and extent of programs that should be undertaken in the areas of recruiting, hiring, job assignment, and performance evaluation. These are the subject matter of Chapter 5.

CHAPTER 5

Filling Jobs and Evaluating Job Performance

Once the present and projected manpower needs of a company are determined through the activities described in Chapter 4, the next requirement for the personnel department is to fill these needs effectively. This is done by recruiting as large a group of applicants as possible with the job skills or training potential for the types of work available, by selecting among these candidates those who are most likely to become productive and successful employees, by placing them in the positions for which they are most suited, and finally by periodically evaluating the job performance of those selected. Information from the performance evaluation can be used both to indicate steps that may be taken to improve performance and to provide feedback for making subsequent selection decisions.

RECRUITING

The goal of the recruiting effort is to provide a steady supply of qualified candidates to fill immediate and future job openings. The extent of a company's recruiting effort and the recruiting sources used depend on the numbers and types of jobs to be filled and on the labor market conditions prevailing in a particular locality or within an industry. Most large employers maintain a continuous recruiting program utilizing several different sources to provide a constant flow of applicants for various types of work. Small firms, particularly those with little turnover in the work force, recruit infrequently—only when there is a specific job opening and no one within the company to fill it.

An important aspect of recruiting involves public relations, especially community relations. A company with a favorable reputation in the local area usually has an easier time finding new employees than companies that do not bother with such matters. At the same time, the way applicants are treated in the employment office or over the telephone can influence the company's image in the community. A paradoxical situation in most personnel offices is that when unemployment is high and there are the fewest jobs to be filled, the number of applicants is greatest. Some companies have had to assign additional staff to the employment office just to process the applications. Even when no jobs are available immediately, if applicants are not treated courteously and letters of application are not answered promptly, future recruiting efforts may suffer.

Another increasingly important part of the recruiting process is providing some system for keeping track of the applications of individuals available for employment. Because of the various FEP laws and regulations, files also need to be kept on applicants who have been considered for a specific job opening and turned down, with a notation of the reason for rejection. Other information that is useful includes records of which recruiting sources are most successful in producing candidates for specific types of jobs. "Successful" in this instance does not necessarily mean merely producing the largest number of candidates; it means producing qualified candidates who later become the better employees in terms of performance and tenure. With this knowledge it is easier to decide which among the several available recruiting sources to turn to when job openings occur.

In-House Recruiting Sources

When a job is to be filled at any point above the beginning or entry level, the present workforce often is the best recruiting source. As noted in Chapter 4, many companies encourage a promotion-from-within policy and use their employee information system to implement this policy. Job vacancies may be publicized throughout the company, in the employee newspaper or by bulletin board notices; this latter technique of "posting" job vacancies is a common requirement in union contracts. One difficulty in unionized operations, however, is that many contracts specify that seniority, or an employee's length of service with the company or in a particular work group, should be the deciding factor if two or more employees bid for the same job, as long as both meet certain minimum qualifications. Thus, it is not always possible to choose the *best* qualified candidate for the job.

Another problem in implementing the recruitment-from-within approach is that a supervisor may be reluctant to recommend one of his employees for promotion or transfer because he does not want to lose one of his best performers and face the necessity of finding and training a replacement. An employee also may be reluctant to apply for a job opening in a different department for fear that if he gets turned down, his supervisor will be angry at his indicating a desire to transfer. Both these problems can be attacked through supervisory training and communication efforts, although it may take time to achieve the desired results.

Unsolicited, "walk-in" job applicants may supply all the candidates needed for jobs to be filled from the outside. This is most likely to be the case where most of the openings, except in entry-level jobs, are filled from within or where the unemployment rate is very high. As mentioned above, however, unsolicited letters or walk-in applicants are likely to be most numerous when new employees are needed the least. For this reason, most employers do try to develop other recruiting sources to call on when the labor market becomes tight.

Employee referrals are considered one of the best sources of recruits in many companies. To encourage such referrals, employees sometimes are offered special incentives such as cash awards or company merchandise for each person recruited who is subsequently hired. Relying on employee referrals may present some hazards in employee relations if an employee's friends or relatives are often turned down for a job. This problem can be minimized if all referrals are given the same consideration and employee referrals are treated the same as all other job applicants. Relying *solely* on employee referrals can result in difficulties with FEP agencies; if a firm's present workforce is 99 percent white, middle-class, and Christian, there are not likely to be many referrals among blacks, disadvantaged, or Jewish members of the community.

An additional in-house recruiting source is that of former employees who want to come back to the labor market, or who return to the area, or who become disenchanted with another employer. As in the case of recruiting from within, more information is available on such candidates, and some companies keep a separate file of former employees they would be willing to rehire. One large New York bank found that among its clerical workers the turnover rate was lowest for reemployed former employees.

Outside Recruiting Sources

While the inside recruiting sources often produce the best prospects and are the least expensive recruiting methods, most companies have to rely on outside sources at one time or another. Large employers and firms undergoing rapid expansion may use all available sources, inside and outside, for periods of time.

Advertising for job applicants, for either a specific opening or for recruits in general, is the most frequently used outside method. The advertisements may be placed directly by the employer or by an employment agency, and they may appear in the local newspaper or in specialized publications such as trade and professional journals to reach people with certain qualifications. One difficulty with a company advertising job openings directly is that it may be flooded with applications long after the job is filled. This is one reason many employers, especially smaller ones, do most of their outside recruiting through an employment agency.

Private employment agencies often save time for both the employer and the applicant. For lower-level positions, the job seeker usually pays the agency fee; for higher-level or hard-to-fill positions, the employer often pays the fee. But the cost may well be less than the expense of advertising and maintaining a staff to handle the applications. Some companies use agencies for all their outside recruiting, while others use them only for jobs requiring special skills. In either case, the agency often performs the initial interviewing and/or testing of applicants before referring them to the employer. For this approach to be really successful, the agency needs to have a clear picture of the company's job structure and of the specific requirements of the jobs to be filled.

Executive search firms are a type of private employment agency used for filling top-level management jobs; these firms sometimes operate as components of management consulting firms. Executive recruiters often are paid a fee for their search whether the candidates they produce are hired or not; as a result this is an expensive type of recruiting. In instances where the company wants to avoid embarrassment to the various persons under consideration, the discretion with which the executive recruiter operates usually is considered worth the expense.

The United States Employment Service (USES), with over 2,000 public employment offices throughout the country, offers a number of recruiting services at no cost to either employer or job applicant.

Use of the public employment offices is widespread—among the companies represented on BNA's *Personnel Policies Forum*, three quarters are reported to use the USES as a recruiting source on a regular basis. The USES also provides assistance to employers in setting up various manpower programs.

A major advantage of the USES is that it is a nationwide operation and can help find people with skills not available locally. A current project of the USES is the development of a nationwide computerized "job bank" system that will provide a daily printout of all job openings listed. Regional job banks already are in operation in several cities.

Recruiting at Schools and Colleges

Schools in the local area—public high schools, trade schools, business machine training schools, community colleges—are a valuable source of recruits for employers with continuing needs for beginning-level manual or clerical workers. Such companies often develop extensive programs aimed at establishing good relationships with teachers and school officials, especially placement and vocational guidance counselors. These programs may include tours of various company plants and offices for both school personnel and students, talks before student groups by company representatives, and the distribution of recruiting brochures and other information booklets about the company.

Work-study programs are another method of recruiting through the local schools. These programs typically provide for part-time employment of students recommended by their schools with the anticipation that they will become full-time employees upon graduation. In the work-study program, most of the training is on the job. In other programs company representatives may provide classroom training at the school, or the company may lend the school some of its equipment for use in teaching certain skills. Summer employment programs serve the recruiting goal in a similar manner.

College recruiting on a regional or national level became a widespread practice in the 1950s when shortages of college-trained engineers and scientists became critical. Now these recruiting efforts are aimed at business administration students, especially in accounting, and those in liberal arts as well, and the graduates hired often go into special management trainee programs. Most on-campus college recruiting programs are extensive and costly and as a result are conducted primarily by larger companies. Even with extensive efforts, however, the results are not always satisfactory. One employer who found that there was a high rate of turnover, especially during the first two years, among employees hired directly off campus discontinued on-campus recruiting and concentrated on graduates with one to three years of experience.

Intern programs for college students, similar to the work-study programs for high school students, have been successful for many companies. The program may involve part-time or summer employment, and it sometimes includes scholarship aid for the student or fellowship support for research at his college. There usually is a commitment to hire the participating student as a regular employee after his graduation if he does well. One study shows that the type of work given the student may determine whether he actually will become a permanent employee. Summer interns given job duties similar to regular employees were much more likely to return after graduation than those assigned to special "make-work" projects.

Other Recruiting Sources

In special circumstances, or for particular types of workers, other outside sources may be called upon. In a few industries, particularly those involving casual labor, the union may be the predominant source of new hires. For specific professional experience or qualifications, trade associations or professional societies may be the best source.

Increasing pressures to offer employment to the disadvantaged or minority-group members have led employers to local civic action groups and churches, as well as to schools and government agencies involved in training programs for such individuals. Some employers also have undertaken special programs for hiring the handicapped, through the Office of Vocational Rehabilitation of the U. S. Department of Health, Education and Welfare; older workers, through the USES; former mental patients, through Veteran's Administration hospitals; or ex-prisoners, through the U. S. Bureau of Prisons.

SELECTION TECHNIQUES

Assuming a company's recruiting programs have been effective, the personnel department should be in a position to consider a number of qualified candidates for each job to be filled. This is the desired situation—to be able to make a decision as to which of several applicants seems likely to become the most successful employee. This decision is made on the basis of various selection techniques; depending on the nature of the position in question, the selection process may take only a day or two or it may require several months.

The Employment Interview

Nearly all prospective employees are interviewed at least once by someone in the personnel office, and candidates for some positions may be interviewed by a number of different people before being offered a job. In small companies, or for certain types of jobs, the interview may be the chief selection device used, whereas in larger companies or for jobs requiring special qualifications, the interview is usually only one factor in the selection decision.

Compared with some of the other selection techniques, the interview has often been criticized as being unscientific. It is not likely to diminish in importance, however, because it does permit exchange of information between the applicant and the company representative. Often the interview provides the best opportunity to determine whether an individual is the type of person who will fit in with the company or with a particular work group and for the applicant to find out if the type of work available is what he is looking for.

In terms of timing, interviews occur at various stages of the selection process. The initial interview, at the time an applicant first comes to the employment office, may be used as a preliminary screening device. Only if the interviewer determines that the person may qualify for present or future job openings is he asked to fill out an application form or take any required tests. If the application information and test results indicate the candidate meets the basic job requirements, there may be an evaluative interview to obtain additional information and to make a judgment as to whether the interviewer would recommend hiring. At this point, the supervisor or department head may interview all the candidates recommended by the personnel department for a specific opening. This is the normal procedure for all jobs where the supervisor makes the final decision regarding whether the applicant should be offered the job.

Different interviewing methods may be used, but for most selection purposes a structured approach appears to work best. Where more than one interviewer is involved, judgments are more likely to be consistent when the same pattern or structure is used by all. The areas to be covered in the interview may be listed, with the interviewer determining the order and wording of the questions, or a standardized detailed interview form or checklist may be used. In either case, it is important for the interviewer to make an evaluation of the applicant as soon as possible after the interview. Many companies use interview evaluation forms for situations where a candidate (usually for higher level positions) is interviewed by several managers. The form usually asks for a rating of qualities such as appearance, poise, maturity, self-confidence, and so forth and includes a question as to whether the interviewer would recommend the applicant for hiring.

Even with the structured approach, interviewing is not an easy task for many supervisors and managers. Large companies often are able to hire full-time interviewers with professional training in interviewing skills for the personnel office. To help supervisors in these companies, and both the personnel staff and supervisors in smaller firms, there are a number of booklets or guides to interviewing available as well as workshops and other training sessions offered by various associations.

Application Blanks

The normal procedure for obtaining information on an applicant's background to use in making a selection decision is to have him fill out an application blank. Forms for this purpose vary from index-card size with a few simple questions to several pages of data, and different forms may be used for different types of jobs. In most companies, the application form is kept as part of the permanent record for each employee hired, for use in connection with future personnel actions.

The type of information requested on the application blank includes identification data (name, address, telephone and social security numbers), personal information such as date of birth and marital status, medical data, education and training completed, job history, military service record, and the names of business, professional, and/or personal references. In some localities, certain types of questions on application forms are prohibited by FEP laws, and in some instances it is permissible to include certain questions but not to use them in making selection decisions. Such limitations apply, for example, to questions about educational level or arrest history, unless there is clear evidence that these matters are related to job performance.

One problem with application blanks is that they tend to grow over the years and may get so long that they discourage people from applying for jobs. Some companies use a short weighted application blank as an initial form. The questions included on such a form are those for which the responses have proved to be valid predictors of subsequent job success. The weight assigned to each response is determined with regard to employees in similar jobs, and the applicants with the highest total scores are considered for that type of job. This technique can be used successfully in situations where there are fairly large numbers of employees performing similar jobs and where continuing studies are made and the weights adjusted accordingly.

Biographical inventories are a more extensive and complicated form of the weighted application blank that has been used by some companies in the selection of office and management personnel, particularly in professional and research operations. The responses are weighted in the same way, but the biographical inventory usually includes a larger number of items and covers matters beyond the usual application form, such as early life experiences, attitudes, interests, and so forth. In some instances, they come close to being a psychological test and are scored similarly.

Checking References

Most employers try to verify some of the information in the application blank by checking with employers, teachers, or other individuals listed as references by the applicant. A check with previous employers is particularly important; it has been found that the information supplied by the job applicant often is inaccurate with regard to time spent in previous employment, reasons for leaving, and rate of payment. Sometimes discrepancies occur between information on the application blank and information turned up during an interview with the applicant. Such matters often can be resolved quickly by a telephone call to the employer involved.

Telephone checks are used more frequently than letters because they are quicker and may yield better information. Employers prefer to check all the information before making a hiring decision rather than getting into the awkward position of receiving a damaging report after the individual is already on the payroll. To make sure that specific points are covered, some companies use a telephone check form. The telephone check may be followed by a written request for information on job titles and pay levels to provide a confirmed record for the personnel files. Schools and colleges often require a signed request before they will send a former student's transcript. Some employers also refuse to supply information without a signed statement by the former employee.

The most valid information obtained through reference checks appears to come from former supervisors rather than from teachers, personal friends, or others who may be listed by the applicant. For the majority of jobs, a check with one or two former supervisors may be sufficient. For certain types of jobs, both in government and in industry, intensive field investigations of an applicant's background are conducted before he is considered for a job. These involve interviews with a variety of people who have known the applicant as well as a detailed check into his financial and credit background.

In some companies consumer credit reports on all job applicants are obtained as a routine step in the hiring process. If the information contained in a credit report is used as the basis for denying a job, however, the applicant is required by law to be notified of this fact, and if a field investigation is to be undertaken, the applicant has to be notified ahead of time.

Preemployment Testing

The selection techniques discussed to this point focus primarily on information related to an applicant's past that will help indicate whether he has the necessary skills, training, or experience for a particular job. Preemployment testing programs, on the other hand, provide information on current performance that can be used to predict aspects of an applicant's future performance on a particular job. From an interview, the application blank, or a reference check, it can be determined that an applicant has had a certain amount of training and experience as a typist, for example, but his present typing ability can be best measured by a test. His performance on the test should indicate the job level for which he is most suited.

The relative importance of a test or set of tests in making selection decisions depends on the job requirements. Where a certain skill or level of ability is necessary to perform a job, applicants may be required to take a test measuring their ability before being given further consideration. In this instance, the test is used as an initial screening device. For many tests used in selection, however, there is no question of passing or failing. The test results merely indicate whether one applicant is likely to perform better, learn faster, or be more loyal than another. The weight given to the test results will depend on the validity of the test in terms of performance on a particular job and, as a practical matter, on how many applicants are available to fill the job.

The following categories indicate the general qualities which are most frequently measured by tests:

Abilities—These are measures of general intelligence, of aptitudes such as spatial or mechanical, and of specific abilities such as dexterity and coordination. The most commonly used are tests measuring general intelligence, which can be applicable to any job. Many firms use a multi-ability battery of several different tests such as the General Aptitude Test Battery (GATB) developed by the USES. Because ability tests usually are not based on specific skills or job knowledge, they are useful in predicting an applicant's potential for jobs that will include on-the-job training.

Skills and achievements—These measures are closely related to a particular job or job category. They may consist of a job sample of the actual work involved, or they may consist of questions to be answered orally or in written form. Large employers often develop their own skill tests, but many firms use the trade tests and work-sample tests developed by the USES. For the small firm, the USES measures have the advantage of having been studied previously with very large groups of workers in various skill categories.

Personality, character, and interests—These measure aspects of the applicant's character that may be related to his work motivation, dependability, self-confidence, maturity, and so forth. There has been considerable controversy over the use of this type of psychological test in the employment situation; in many instances, the applicant is not aware of what personality characteristics are being measured. A large amount of research has been and is being done on relationships between measures of personality characteristics and job performance, however. In many instances these measures have been found to be quite reliable and effective, notably in the selection of managers and salesmen.

The installation and administration of a testing program is one area where the personnel department requires professional assistance. This may be provided by psychologists on the staff, by private outside consultants, or through the USES. Particularly in view of the pressures from FEP agencies to make sure tests are job-related, the validation of each test used is essential. This can be done most effectively by someone with professional experience in psychological tests and measurement. Methods of validating tests and other selection techniques will be discussed in the next section of this chapter.

Physical examinations are related to psychological testing as a selection device in that they provide an estimate of an applicant's future effectiveness by measuring his present state of functioning. However, the physical exam rarely is the basis for rejecting an otherwise qualified applicant. Usually it is the last step in the selection process, and sometimes it does not occur until after an employee has actually been hired, unless the job requires specific physical abilities. For some jobs, certain truck drivers for example, government regulations require a physical exam and set specific standards in such categories as vision. To screen out applicants with any physical problems that might lead to disqualification for a particular job, some companies require the completion of a medical checklist as part of the application form.

SELECTION DECISIONS

The final decision as to whether a particular applicant is to be offered a job or whether an employee is to be selected for promotion is an important matter for both parties. The decision may affect the applicant's entire future, and companies frequently take this into account in making selection decisions. They look for candidates who not only have the qualifications to fill a specific job vacancy but who also are the type of individuals most likely to have long successful careers with the firm. The fact of change—in people, jobs, organizations, and over time—makes such decision-making extremely difficult. However, certain procedures have been developed for evaluating the information obtained through the various selection techniques.

Validating Selection Techniques

The type of procedure most frequently used for measuring the effectiveness of a selection technique is known as *validation;* validation was developed originally with reference to psychological testing. The validation process may involve complex statistical calculations, and the computer increasingly is being used as an aid.

Basically, however, what is required is that a study be made to determine whether there is any significant relationship (in a statistical sense) between an item of preemployment data and job success. There are two methods commonly used in making such studies, concurrent and longitudinal. In the case of the validation of a particular psychological test, for example, this is how the two methods would work:

Concurrent method—Give the test to a group of employees on the job; rate the employees on the basis of some aspect of job performance such as productivity, or on the basis of several factors; compare the test scores of the higher-rated employees against those of lower-rated employees. If there appears to be a correlation, the test may be valid for that specific job.

Longitudinal method—Give the test to prospective employees at the time of hiring, but do not use the results as a basis for hiring. When a large enough number of tested new hires have been on the job a reasonable length of time, rate them as in the concurrent method and compare the test scores with the ratings.

In both methods, a second study, called a *cross-validation,* should be undertaken whenever there appears to be a significant relationship. The cross-validation is done using a different group of employees or applicants but in the same job and using the same performance measures. This is to make sure the relationship found with the first group is not merely a chance fluctuation. Ideally the cross-validation should be done at a different point in time, although this is not always possible when there are time and cost pressures involved.

Similar validation studies can be made with respect to other preemployment data. They can be used for items available in the personnel files of the employees on the job, such as interviewers' ratings, biographical data, and so forth. They can be used for any item or technique that appears to have a performance relationship for a particular job and that the personnel staff wishes to study. Because most jobs involve a number of skill and behavioral aspects, there usually are several items of information or selection techniques that prove to be valid predictors of job success. These multiple predictors may be combined in a number of ways to provide a scale or a profile against which an applicant's score or scores can be measured. In recent years, a number of computerized selection procedures have been developed utilizing as many as 40 or 50 different items of information. These so-called "broadband" techniques have proved particularly effective in the selection of employees to be promoted into higher level management positions.

Two kinds of information are necessary for carrying out effective validation of selection techniques. The first has to do with the specifications of a job, or a group of related jobs. In order to make an initial determination of what preemployment data might have validity, such specifications as whether a job requires individual initiative or depends mostly on following orders, or whether the job requires a certain level of education or experience or a specific ability such as being able to drive a truck, need to be analyzed. These specifications are readily available in companies with standardized job analysis procedures. In situations where standardized specifications are not available for a particular job, the supervisor may be asked to fill out a checklist of qualifications for the job.

In many companies, particularly small ones, where few vacancies occur in any one job category, the job specification is the only information obtained. The selection process then is based on hunch or intuition rather than on validation. This is not entirely unreasonable in many situations—if a job requires typing ability it would seem appropriate to make a selection decision on the basis of a typing test. And if only one or two job vacancies a year involve typing, it would take years to have a large enough sample of employees to conduct a validity study on this particular job requirement.

Many employers have relied on standardized tests available commercially or through the USES that have been validated on larger numbers of persons in a particular job category than would be available to most single employers. However, it is increasingly clear that any employer large enough to be subject to FEP regulations also needs to validate any selection tests used with respect to his own specific group of employees. In order to accomplish this, it is essential to provide the second kind of information referred to above. This information relates to the evaluation and appraisal of job performance and the development of *criteria* for measuring the match between preemployment data and job behavior.

PERFORMANCE APPRAISAL

Throughout the discussion in this chapter we have referred to the types of individuals who appear to be most likely to become effective employees. We have considered the recruiting sources—

where such individuals might be located—and the selection techniques that aid in determining exactly which individuals they might be. But we have not indicated the basis for specifying what is and what is not considered effective or successful job performance. Before discussing the various methods of measuring employee performance and the difficulties associated with each, it should be noted that most companies carry on performance appraisal activities for a large number of purposes. The granting of a wage increase, for example, typically is based on the appraisal of an employee's performance by his supervisor. In fact, many companies that have not conducted validity studies of their selection techniques have programs for evaluating employee performance, particularly at the managerial level.

Measures of Job Performance

In the absence of a formal program for supervisory rating of employee performance on a judgmental basis, objective measures can provide a basis for developing selection criteria. Examples of objective measures include quantity of work, as measured by number of units produced or volume of sales; quality of work, as measured by number of rejects or errors, or by customer comments; and job attitudes, as measured by absenteeism, or complaints, or grievances filed. For employees below managerial rank these measures are evaluated on an individual basis. For managers the evaluation is based on the performance of the subordinate work group or department and may include profit figures, data on employee turnover, and results of employee attitude surveys as well.

In using this type of information for personnel actions, standards may be established as a basis for comparison. The employee's absence rate, for example, may be compared against his own past performance, against that of other individuals in the same work group, against that the company as a whole, or against a previously established minimum standard of satisfactory or unsatisfactory performance.

In general, the objective measures of performance do not present the difficulties that arise with judgmental measures. For one thing, it is relatively easy to determine whether or not a particular measure, such as volume of sales, is actually related to job performance. However, there are many jobs for which performance cannot easily be determined on the basis of objective measures alone; reliance on objective measures of performance might even result in poor performance in the long run. A manager evaluated solely on the basis of sales results may neglect such responsibilities as developing his subordinates or maintaining discipline. It is for this reason that nearly all companies with a formal performance appraisal program use some form of judgmental evaluation, either alone or in conjunction with objective measures.

Rating Systems

Most judgmental performance evaluations involve some type of rating system. These range from a simple one-factor judgment of the employee's overall performance as outstanding, average, or unsatisfactory to an appraisal of 20 to 30 different factors related to the employee's skills in various areas, his personal traits and behavior patterns, and his potential. Rating systems based on a number of factors may be viewed as more or less behaviorally specific.

A rating system with a high degree of behavioral specificity is one in which the rating measure itself incorporates descriptions of actual or desired job behavior. For rating sales personnel, for example, the evaluation form might include an item relating to effectiveness in dealing with customers. The descriptions of behavior used in the rating form are derived from the job description resulting from the process of job analysis. All elements of the job description may be used or only those determined to be most closely associated with a high level of performance.

Highly behaviorally specific rating systems are time-consuming and costly; separate rating forms are needed for each job or group of similar jobs. While such systems usually are viewed as preferable, there is strong evidence that less behaviorally specific measures may be just as effective for many purposes. A major advantage is that the same rating form can be used for a great variety of jobs if it is based on global characteristics such as cooperativeness and potential for promotion.

Rating Methods

No matter what the degree of behavioral specificity of the rating system, a number of methods may be used in the rating process.

Rating scales provide a scale of several degrees, ranging from poor to excellent or from unsatisfactory to outstanding, on which the employee is evaluated for each factor such as dependability, cooperation, and so forth. Under the employee comparison system, the rater ranks all employees in a particular group on the basis of overall performance or on the basis of specific factors. The ranking may be done directly, by comparing the performance of each individual in the group with every other individual, or by a forced distribution in which employees in the group are designated as being in specific categories of performance. Such a distribution might be the top 10 percent (those viewed as the best performers), next 20 percent, middle 40 percent, next 20 percent, and lowest 10 percent. Other rating methods include the use of a checklist on which the rater checks the characteristics applicable to the employee from a list of job behaviors, and the essay evaluation, in which the rater writes answers to two or three questions concerning the employee's strengths and weaknesses, potential for advancement, and the like. A number of other rating methods have been developed within specific companies.

One reason for the large variety of methods used to rate performance is that the subjective nature of the process results in several possible sources of error or bias. These include such phenomena as the "halo" effect, in which an employee viewed as good or outstanding on one dimension is likely to be rated as a high performer on all dimensions, the tendency to rate employees on the basis of their most recent behavior, and outright bias, whether conscious or not. To overcome these problems, appraisals often are made by two or more superiors. The evidence indicates that such multiple evaluations are clearly preferable to single appraisals. It is not always possible, however, to find two or more superiors familiar enough with the manager's or employee's work to make a competent evaluation of his performance. In this situation, a series of evaluations may be made over a period of time by a single superior and the results averaged to produce the final appraisal. In some instances, peers or subordinates are asked to make appraisals of managers' performance to supplement the superior's rating.

Another problem with performance appraisal systems is that different managers often have different standards, and an employee judged to be performing "satisfactorily" by one superior may be rated as "outstanding" by another. This problem may be reduced by the use of multiple raters. Another approach is the field review. This involves the use of appraisal specialists, either from the personnel department or outside consultants, who collect the performance data orally from the superior and write up the appraisal on the basis of similar standards applied throughout the company.

Appraisal by Results

In an attempt to eliminate some of the problems of bias and the emphasis on personal judgment inherent in many rating systems, a number of companies have adopted an appraisal-by-results system. Often this is tied in with the management-by-objectives approach mentioned in Chapter 4. In this system, the performance appraisal is confined to how well the manager has met certain predetermined goals or objectives established at the time of a previous appraisal.

Appraisal by results developed in part because of the difficulty experienced by many managers in feeding back appraisal data to their subordinates. In some cases it was found that the superiors never did discuss the appraisal results with the employees; in other cases it was determined that the ratings came out higher when there was a feedback requirement. In both instances the appraisal program was not being used effectively as a means of improving employee performance; goal-planning sessions yielded better results.

Using Appraisal Data

Because of the multiple uses of appraisal information, several approaches may be preferable to one. The appraisal-by-results system, for example, may not provide the type of stable data that is most useful for developing selection criteria even though it has been quite effective as a management development tool. It seems clear that an overall appraisal based on a number of objective measures and judgments derived from multiple sources is superior to an appraisal based on only one or two measures. Such an overall appraisal would appear to be most appropriate for use in the validation of selection techniques.

The management-assessment-center approach is an example of an appraisal system using multiple sources. The individual is assessed on the basis of personal history data, interviews with several different managers, results of performance on a number of situational exercises, psychological tests, and peer evaluations. The end result is a composite rating with particular reference to the employee's potential for success in higher level management positions. Because the assessment center is a costly procedure—both the individuals being appraised and the managers doing the rating lose several days from their regular jobs in the process—its use has been restricted for the most part to very large corporations. Smaller firms may be able to achieve somewhat similar assessments by combining performance ratings from a variety of sources with test and personal data.

One important use of appraisal data is to indicate areas where the employee or manager may need additional training or development to perform his job satisfactorily, to improve his performance, or to be prepared for moving into more demanding jobs. The assessment center and most other management appraisal summaries include a discussion of the employee's strengths and weaknesses, and one reason for the feedback of appraisal information is to encourage employees to take steps to correct their weaknesses and thus improve their performance. The types of programs available to employees to accomplish this are the subject of the next chapter.

Chapter 6

Training and Development

Training or employee development activities are carried on in all organizations in some degree. They may be limited to the office manager's showing a new typist where supplies are kept and how to fill out a time card, or they may be as broad as an organizational development effort requiring all managers to spend several weeks in a laboratory training setting. Training programs are conducted in co-operation with local schools and manpower agencies, by outside specialists in industrial education or management development, by company training staffs, and by schools or institutes established by the company itself.

TRAINING GOALS AND METHODS

The ultimate goal of any training activity is to contribute to improved employee performance, whether this is measured by a higher level of productivity or by a more favorable attitude toward the company. In terms of the model of the personnel function outlined in Chapter 1, training activities come under the heading of input-mediators. Their purpose usually is to improve upon the quality of the personnel selected to fill the jobs in the organization. For some jobs, it may not be possible to find applicants with the necessary mix of skill and experience; this situation calls for a major emphasis on training rather than selection. The selection criteria then would be based on ability to learn rather than on ability to perform a specific job.

In more specific terms, training goals may be one or more of the following—

—to teach employees how to perform a new or unfamiliar job.

This is the goal of on-the-job training for newly hired employees and of preemployment training programs such as those aimed at helping the hard-core unemployed or disadvantaged.

—to prepare employees to move into new positions. These programs may involve retraining because of the elimination of certain jobs, or they may be part of a planned career ladder or promotion-from-within policy.

—to help employees improve their performance. These programs may involve updating of skills and/or subject knowledge, they may be individual self-development efforts, or they may involve attempts to change attitudes. Management development and organizational change programs are of this variety.

Training Needs and Program Evaluation

In any large organization, many different training programs will be going on at any one point in time depending on the needs of the various work groups and departments. To determine exactly what types of training programs should be undertaken, companies may make a training-needs analysis. This contains information from several sources—job analysis and organization planning data indicate the training requirements for specific jobs and positions; manpower planning and employee information system data point to potential surpluses or shortages of particular skills; performance appraisals specify the training or development needs of individual employees. Other inputs to a training-needs analysis come from top management, which may be considering a major expansion or an effort to change the organizational climate. In addition, the personnel or training department may make a periodic survey among supervisors using a checklist of items, such as the work unit's safety record, that might be improved with some type of training.

Once a comprehensive list of training needs is available, it is necessary to establish priorities since the variety of programs that would help improve the performance of one employee or another is almost endless. The training of new employees and of present employees for new jobs usually receives the highest priority and is maintained on a continuing basis. For other training programs, however, it is necessary to decide among several alternatives depending on how many employees would benefit from a particular program and the costs and availability of such programs. In most instances, costs are a major factor, and it is an unfortunate fact that when a company has financial problems the training program typically is the first personnel area to be cut back.

When it has been decided to undertake a particular training effort, and the funds are available, there still is the question of what is the most effective method for achieving the desired training goals. This is not too difficult a problem for skill training. Most companies have standard procedures for this type of training, and the results can be easily measured by such factors as an increase in production or a decrease in errors. The results of many supervisory training programs can be measured by changes in such things as the number of employee complaints or grievances, or by absenteeism and turnover rates.

For many types of programs, including some supervisory training and most management and organizational development efforts, it is far more difficult to measure the results. Nor is it always possible to determine that when there are changes in the desired direction they are necessarily the result of the training—it may be that the changes would have occurred even in the absence of any special effort. To answer these questions, the training program can be validated in a manner similar to the validation of selection tests.

The usual procedure for validating a training program is to select two groups of employees or managers with the same general characteristics and give them some measure relating to the goals of the proposed program. The measure may concern some aspect of job knowledge, or it may be an attitude questionnaire or a test of work motivation, depending on the type of program involved. One group—the experimental group—is given the training, while the other group—the control group—is not. At some later point in time, both groups are given the measure again. If there is a statistically significant change in the test results of the experimental group as compared with the control group, it is presumed that the training was effective. As in the case of test validation, this is a time-consuming process and is warranted only where a fairly large number of employees are to be trained in a particular way.

For the majority of training situations, companies rely on their own or other employers' past experiences in deciding the programs to undertake and the methods to be used. Occasionally, trainees are asked their opinions after completing a program, but the participants' liking it does not really say anything about its effectiveness. More reliable information may come from supervisors' appraisals after the employees have been back on the job for a period of time after the training.

Training in Job Skills

The major component of the training effort in most companies relates to teaching employees how to perform the jobs for which they were hired. As an initial step, new employees may undergo a program of *orientation* training on either a formal or an informal basis. At a minimum the new employee is introduced to his supervisor and other workers in the group, told what he is expected to do, and shown his work station and where to get tools, supplies, or other items he may need to perform his job. Sometimes an experienced employee is assigned as a "buddy" or sponsor for the new employee for a period of time. A number of companies have elaborate orientation programs, using lectures, slides, and films to depict company rules and regulations, employee benefits and services, company history, organization, and products, and so forth. At some firms, employees receive a short orientation at the time of hire and a longer program when they have completed a probationary period and are considered permanent employees.

On-the-Job Training—The most common approach to teaching job skills is basically a learn-by-doing method referred to as on-the-job training, or OJT. OJT can be a very informal process in which the employee gradually becomes familiar with the machinery and materials with help from his supervisor or fellow employees. For many jobs, a more formal approach is followed involving training instructors and using the Job Instruction Training (JIT) guidelines developed by the War Manpower Commission during World War II, as mentioned in Chapter 2. The major problem with on-the-job training arises in factory situations where there are risks that inexperienced workers might cause accidents or damage to equipment. This is one reason for the use of off-the-job techniques.

Coaching—One type of OJT is the coach-pupil method, often called the buddy system. It is similar to the orientation approach noted above. This approach consists of assigning an old hand to coach the new employee for as long a time as necessary.

Job Rotation—Once an employee has mastered one job, he may be given an opportunity for on-the-job training in one or more related jobs as a means of broadening his experience and skill. Such job rotation often is used to train employees for promotion.

Vestibule Training—In vestibule training, employees are put through a short course under simulated shop or office conditions. Trainees use the same equipment and procedures as they would in on-the-job training, but the equipment is set up in an area separate from the regular work place. Thus there is no interference with actual production, and the new employee is able to do the work required the first day he begins in the normal workplace.

Apprenticeship—Training in an apprenticeship program is a formal approach used for skilled occupations that lasts from two to six years, depending on the degree of skill required. Most apprenticeship programs are sponsored jointly by a company and a union and are supervised by the U.S. Department of Labor. In addition to on-the-job experience, apprentices in registered programs receive a minimum of 144 hours of classroom instruction per year.

Teaching Machines and Programmed Instruction—The use of electronic teaching machines or programmed textbooks is a more recent development in industrial training than the approaches listed above. Their use is widespread, however, and there are one or more programmed learning courses for most common job categories in the plant or office. Based on principles of learning developed and tested by educational psychologists, notably B.F. Skinner, of Harvard University, programmed instruction is an individualized approach in which the material to be learned is organized into a set of frames. The frames, which are presented in a machine using film or sound tape or printed in a booklet, are of increasing difficulty with each one building on those that precede it. Information, questions, and problems are presented to the trainee, and he is provided feedback on the correctness of his answers.

Although the initial costs of producing a programmed text or tape are extremely high, the use of such programs has several advantages. Because employees can complete the program on their own time and at their own pace, employers often encourage the use of these programs to prepare employees for promotion to higher level positions.

Lecture or Classroom Methods—For some types of training, where a large amount of information has to be given to a large group of employees in a short period of time, a lecture or some other classroom approach is often most appropriate. This might be the case, for example, where a company changes its procedures for handling orders or introduces a new kind of equipment. The oral presentation may be supplemented by a variety of visual aids such as charts, posters, slides, films, and videotape, and there usually is an opportunity for discussion and questions from employees.

Conferences—Conferences, usually limited to 10 to 15 participants, involve controlled or directed discussions of an informal nature. This approach is most effective as a training device where the discussion is conducted by an informed leader and where the topic is one that will benefit from ideas of and acceptance among members of the group. The company safety engineer might use the conference method for showing employees how to use a new safety device and for obtaining suggestions on how to improve the company's accident rate at the same time.

Training for the Disadvantaged

In recent years, employers have been under increasing pressure to provide employment opportunities for minority group members, the culturally disadvantaged in particular. This has resulted in a number of new kinds of training programs, most of them financed at least in part with funds available under the federal Manpower Development and Training Act (MDTA). When the MDTA was first enacted in 1962, it was aimed at providing retraining for workers unemployed as a result of technological change. It became clear, however, that while automation was not causing extensive unemployment among experienced workers, there was a "hard core" of unemployed persons even when jobs were plentiful. Most of the MDTA programs now are aimed at providing whatever training is needed to help these hard-core unemployable individuals move into the labor force.

At present, there are a wide variety of federally assisted manpower development programs for the disadvantaged. In the private sector, the most significant of the programs is JOBS (Job Opportunities in the Business Sector); Public Service Careers is a similar program for government employment. JOBS is sponsored by the National Alliance of Businessmen (NAB), which was formed in 1968 as a result of the resistance the government encountered in attempting to establish on-the-job training programs for the disadvantaged even with MDTA financing.

One of the difficulties in training the culturally disadvantaged is that a lot more than just training in basic job skills seems to be required before such individuals become effective employees. The more successful programs have included counseling and other types of individual assistance, including help with personal problems, and have covered such topics as grooming and hygiene, getting along

with others, money management, use of public transportation facilities, and orientation to the world of work. Special training for supervisors involved also contributes to the effectiveness of these programs.

Self-Development Programs

In addition to training programs required as part of the job and
directly related to the job, educational efforts aimed at self-
development are offered or encouraged by many companies. High
school or college-level courses may be taught on company premises
and even on company time in some instances; subject matter may be
limited to topics related to present or future job aspects or may
cover any topic an employee shows an interest in. Adult education
courses for employees who never received a high school diploma
have been extended to include job applicants who fail to meet employment standards in some firms.

Tuition-aid plans provide another method for encouraging employee self-development. These plans involve the reimbursement to
the employee of part or all of the cost of college or university, corre-
spondence school, or professional courses taken at the employee's
initiative. Under most plans, the course has to be job related, although the definition of "job related" has broadened over the years;
the amount of reimbursement sometimes is on a sliding-scale basis
according to the grade received in the course.

Supervisory Training

Because the majority of first-level supervisors are promoted
from the ranks, most companies provide some type of special training to ease the transition to the leadership position. The training may
be of an informal nature, and it may occur long before promotion to
the supervisory position. Some companies develop a pool of potential supervisors by designating certain employees to serve as group
leaders, or having them fill in on the supervisor's day off or during
his vacation, or help him break in new employees. Most large companies also include some classroom instruction for new or potential
supervisors.

Much of the instruction covers topics related to the new or anticipated responsibilities. These include how to write the reports and
keep the records required, how to give new employees on-the-job
training, how to conduct selection and appraisal interviews, how to

make performance evaluations, and how to promote safety, quality control, good housekeeping, and so forth. Communications skills programs and a review of employee relations policies are often provided to help the new supervisor in dealing with employee questions. In unionized situations, the terms of the contract and grievance handling are almost always covered.

Some programs for first-level supervisors are designed to encourage qualities of leadership, to promote good human relations, and to provide opportunities for self-development. These programs are appropriate to all levels of management and are discussed in the section following.

MANAGEMENT DEVELOPMENT

Some type of management development effort is standard in nearly all companies of any size. Because the objective of such programs is to improve the effectiveness of the managerial staff, they may be designed to heighten the participant's creativity, problem-solving ability, achievement motivation, sensitivity to others, or motivation to manage as well as to provide knowledge in areas that relate to his position. These programs often are developed by in-house training staffs in large organizations, but most companies also make use of programs conducted by colleges and universities, by business, trade, or professional associations, and by professional training consultants.

Management Development Techniques

Techniques for the job-related aspects of management development are similar to those for nonmanagerial jobs. They may include job rotation, sometimes over a period of several years, as well as the encouragement of self-development by tuition aid, conferences, and lectures. However, several techniques have been developed for use primarily to help increase management skills. The following are among the most widely used in formal management development programs:

Case Study—Members of the trainee group are given a problem, usually in written form, and they prepare a solution on either an individual or a group basis. This method has been found to be helpful in teaching managers to identify and analyze complex problems and to make their own decisions.

The Incident Process—This method is similar to case study but differs in that the case is developed in a question and answer manner on the basis of a brief written incident. The solutions are worked out in small group discussions and then presented to the entire group, and the actual solution and its consequences are discussed.

Role Playing—With this method, a case study is acted out with some of the trainees playing various roles of the persons in the case and other trainees serving as analysts. This method is used extensively in programs relating to grievance handling and other employee relations problems, and in sales training.

Business Games—These are exercises designed to simulate the operations of an actual business organization or segments of it, such as production scheduling, sales management, collective bargaining, and so forth. Competing teams of trainees make decisions on the basis of information provided. The results of these decisions are calculated (often on a computer) and fed back to the teams. This cycle may be repeated several times, and the final results are discussed at length.

Situational Exercises—These are simulations of decision-making aspects of a manager's actual job. One example is the "in-basket" exercise in which the trainee is given an in-basket filled with various letters, memos, and telephone messages along with some background information on the responsibilities of the job involved in the exercise. He then spends a couple of hours deciding how to handle the material in the basket. An evaluation of his actions and decisions is used to develop his managerial skills. Exercises like this also are used in the selection of management personnel, particularly as part of the assessment-center approach.

Sensitivity Training—Also known as laboratory or T-group training, this is a type of human relations training that is designed to make managers more sensitive to themselves as individuals and in their relationships with others. Groups of 10 or 12 participants meet together for several hours a day for a period of a week or longer. The groups are called "family" laboratories if the participants are all from the same work group or department, "cousin" labs if the participants are all from the same company but different departments, and "stranger" labs if the participants are from different organizations. The goals of this type of training are to make participants value behavioral science, democracy, and helping others more than they have in the past.

Problems in Management Development

Two major difficulties arise in the evaluation of management development programs. One of these is the problem of whether the managers are able to transfer their new skills and knowledge to their situations on the job. It may be that the knowledge acquired in a management training program has no relevance for a particular position or in a particular firm. This situation can occur when the company buys a "canned" program or sends its managers to courses outside without thoroughly investigating the goals and content of the course. An effort should be made to determine whether the change in knowledge or in attitudes that the program aims to produce is actually associated with success in the management job.

The second problem is somewhat related to the first and involves the organization's goals and values. For a manager to benefit from training, the training goals and the organizational goals have to mesh. Many management development efforts, particularly those involving sensitivity training, emphasize consideration for the feelings of others. Having had this type of training, a manager back on the job may find himself in a constant state of conflict if his superiors emphasize only high levels of production. In recognition of this problem, a new process has emerged which involves an effort to change the organization, in terms of its values, attitudes, and structure, from the top down. This type of change effort is known as *organization development*, or OD.

ORGANIZATION DEVELOPMENT

The concept of organization development still is relatively new, and the process itself varies considerably from one organization to another. In most applications, however, there is a planned intervention by an outside consultant, usually a behavioral scientist, and some variant of sensitivity or laboratory training frequently is the primary method used to effect change. The OD effort may require a number of years, or it may be viewed as a continuous process.

Most organization development programs place strong emphasis on participative, democratic procedures with the aim of increased equalization of power. They are based on various concepts and theories of leadership and motivation that have been built up over the past 20 to 30 years by a number of behavioral scientists. The remainder of this chapter will be devoted to a brief summary of the behavioral science concepts that are most widely used as the basis for these management training and organization development efforts.

Likert's "Linking Pin" and "System 4" Concepts

One of the first social psychologists to undertake extensive study of organizational relationships was Rensis Likert, who was director of the Institute for Social Research at the University of Michigan from 1946 until his retirement in 1971. The *linking pin* concept evolved from Likert's research on groups in organizations. The linking pins in organizations are those persons who belong to two overlapping groups. This is true of nearly all managers from first-level supervisor on up; they are the superiors in one group and subordinates in another. To contribute to the effectiveness of the person in the linking-pin position, Likert stresses open communication, development of mutual trust, group goal setting, and shared responsibility—what is often called *participative management*.

More recent research led Likert to the conceptualization of four systems of management based on leadership styles. These are:
System 1—Exploitive-Authoritative leadership
System 2—Benevolent-Authoritative leadership
System 3—Consultative leadership
System 4—Participative-Group leadership
While he recognizes the time and effort needed to achieve it, Likert advocates his "System 4" as being the basis for the most successful and creative organizations.

McGregor's "Theory X and Theory Y"

According to the late Douglas McGregor, Professor of Industrial Management at MIT at the time of his death in 1964, there are differing management styles based on differing views of man. One, which he labelled *Theory X*, assumes that people by nature dislike work, lack ambition, avoid responsibility, and prefer or need to be directed in their work. These assumptions lead to an authoritarian approach to management, in which the individual is shaped to meet the organization's needs and control is externally imposed on the individual by strict management supervision.

Theory Y, on the other hand, is based on the assumptions that people are not passive, have development potential, can learn, can be motivated, and may desire to assume more responsibility.

McGregor's view is that management should try to create an organizational environment in which people can realize their potential for personal growth and achieve their goals by their own efforts. Bascially, McGregor advocates a flexible approach, taking into account situational requirements and the nature of the work force, using authority only where appropriate.

Argyris's "Mix Model"

One of the strongest supporters of the use of laboratory training methods for organization development is Chris Argyris, who was head of Yale's department of administrative sciences for several years and is now at Harvard. Argyris argues that, in most industrial organizations, the needs and goals of individuals are antithetical to those of the organization, and what is needed is a process by which both the individual and the organization change. The desired result is an integration of organizational and individual needs and efforts.

As the basis for determining the extent of change required and in what areas, Argyris developed a *mix model* of six organizational variables which he calls essential properties. These properties relate to the source and balance of power in the organization, the relationship and control between the parts of the organization and the whole, whether objectives are related to the parts or the whole organization, influence over internal factors, influence over external factors, and future growth. Depending on the mix of these properties in an organization, the individual will tend to be alienated from or integrated with the organization.

Argyris also is credited with contributing to the concept of *job enlargement*, and thus expanding job content on a horizontal basis to include a wider range of tasks as well as an interchange of tasks among work group members. This interchange, Argyris says, should improve job knowledge and contribute to group interaction and cohesiveness.

Blake and Mouton's "Managerial Grid"

A device frequently used in organization development programs is the *Managerial Grid*, developed by Robert Blake and Jane Mouton, formerly of the University of Texas and now in private business. The Grid itself is a chart of managerial styles with two nine-point scales; the vertical scale represents concern for people and the horizontal scale represents concern for production. On both scales number one is low concern and number nine is high. Thus, a highly authoritarian manager would rate 9 on concern for production and 1 on concern for people, while the manager concerned primarily with having a happy and harmonious work group would rate just the opposite, or 1, 9. A 1,1 manager is one who doesn't lead at all, and a 5,5 manager tends to compromise between concern with people and concern with production with the result that his performance usually is viewed as mediocre. The ideal is a 9,9 manager who has a maximum concern for both people and production and views them as interdependent.

The Managerial Grid is introduced in a week-long training seminar in which managers assess their own leadership styles as a basis for improvement. The seminar is similar to a sensitivity training session except that the group's discussions are concerned only with work-related problems. Blake and Mouton also have developed programs based on the Grid for organization development efforts extending over a period of several years.

McClelland's "Achievement Motivation" Theory

Research based on personality theory conducted by Harvard psychologist David McClelland and his associates involves the use of a projective test to indicate the strength of certain motives that are related to job performance. The three motives studied by McClelland are the need for achievement (sometimes expressed as n^{ach}), the need for power, and the need for affiliation. For success in business, the achievement motive is considered most important, then power, with affiliation sometimes having negative consequences.

People with high achievement motivation are interested in advancing their careers or accomplishing important things, they work hard when they know there is a reasonably good chance for success, and they desire feedback on how well they are doing. High achievement motivation has been found to be associated with entrepreneurial success, and several management development programs have been undertaken with a view to increasing the achievement motivation among an organization's managers.

Maslow's "Needs Hierarchy"

Another theory of personality and motivation is the *Hierarchy of Needs* developed by the late psychologist Abraham Maslow. Mas-

low's work initially was done with little reference to work motivation, but McGregor drew heavily on Maslow's theory in developing
his concept of Theory Y. Maslow's hierarchy of motives usually is depicted as follows:

> —Need for self-actualization (growth, de-
> velopment, achieving one's full poten-
> tial, creativity, self-fulfillment).

> —Ego needs (both self-esteem as expressed by
> feeling of self-confidence, adequacy, and
> competence; and esteem of others as ex-
> pressed by status, recognition, attention, and
> prestige).

> —Social needs (friendship, affection, love, belonging-
> ness).

> —Safety needs (freedom from bodily harm, protection against
> danger, the feeling of having a predictable, stable, and se-
> cure environment).

—Physiological needs (food, water, shelter, sleep, sexual fulfillment,
and other bodily needs).

According to Maslow, once one level of needs in the hierarchy is satisfied, these needs will no longer provide the motivation for determining behavior. The highest level need of self-actualization, however, never is completely satisfied because it involves growth and a
perpetual process of finding and reaching new goals. Maslow looked
forward to a society populated with superior persons, those whose
lower level needs are satisfied so they can concentrate on creative,
self-actualizing endeavors. He coined the word *eupsychian* to describe this ideal society.

In terms of today's society, at least in the United States, most
people are viewed as having their physiological and safety needs satisfied to a large degree as they grow from infancy to adulthood. In
the world of work, then, the majority of employees can be expected
to be motivated by social, ego, or self-actualization needs. The problem for management is how to determine which of these needs
motivate which employees and under what circumstances.

Herzberg's "Two-Factor" Theory

A theory of work motivation having much in common with Maslow's need hierarchy is the *motivation-hygiene*, or two-factor, the-

ory developed by Frederick Herzberg, formerly of Case Western Reserve University and now of the University of Utah. From research on job attitudes, Herzberg found two classes of job factors related to motivation. These sets of factors, which correspond roughly to the lower and higher level need categories of Maslow's system, are described as follows:

> *Dissatisfiers* (also called extrinsic, hygienic, job context, maintenance, or environmental factors)—
>> company policy and administration
>> technical aspects of supervision
>> working conditions
>> interpersonal relations with superiors, subordinates, and peers
>> salary
>> status
>> job security
>> certain factors affecting personal life
>
> *Satisfiers* (also called intrinsic or job content factors, or motivators)—
>> achievement
>> recognition
>> work itself
>> responsibility
>> advancement
>> growth

The dissatisfiers or extrinsic factors affect job performance only by their absence. Management efforts related to these factors can result in minimizing job dissatisfaction, but they cannot be expected to motivate employees to higher levels of performance. This is accomplished by the satisfiers or intrinsic factors. If the extrinsic factors are neglected, however, the motivators may not operate fully; in effect, employees' lower order needs for such things as good wages and working conditions need to be satisfied so that they can be motivated by opportunities for advancement and recognition.

In implementing his theory of business organizations, Herzberg emphasizes the concepts of *meaningful work* and *job enrichment*. Job enrichment involves increasing the challenging content of a job so that the individual grows in skill, achievement, and recognition. This is accomplished by giving the employee responsibility for planning and controlling many aspects of the job previously handled by superiors. Thus, it involves increasing the vertical responsibilities of the job as compared with job enlargement, which typically involves increasing the horizontal job aspects primarily.

It is clear from the work of these and other behavioral scientists that the questions of leadership style and employee motivation are complex. To date, there are no proved formulas providing "the answer" to guide supervisors and higher level managers in their efforts to motivate employees to higher levels of performance. The best approach at present may be for companies to give their managers an exposure to various behavioral science concepts in their management and organization development programs. On the basis of their own perceptions of their subordinates, the organizational pressures, and the specific task objectives, the manager can decide for himself the motivational approach that appears to have the best chance of succeeding.

While the research indicates that the matter of leadership is the most critical aspect of employee job satisfaction, motivation, and productivity, the other aspects certainly cannot be ignored. As Herzberg points out, neglecting the extrinsic factors will cause dissatisfaction, which can contribute to poor job performance. Furthermore, a firm that does neglect these factors will have a more difficult time attracting competent individuals. Personnel activities related to these factors in the areas of compensation, employee relations and services, safety and working conditions, and communications will be discussed in the next two chapters.

CHAPTER 7

Compensation

The essence of the employment relationship is that the employee is hired to perform work for which he is *paid* by the employer. Thus, some type of compensation program is found in every employing organization, and activities related to such programs make up a large share of the work of the personnel department. As noted in Chapter 3, practices and procedures covering the payment of wages and of benefits are more directly influenced by outside factors than are those in any other area of personnel.

Because of the outside influences—legal requirements, union pressures for "more," and labor market conditions—most companies have concentrated on economic factors in establishing their wage and salary programs. The primary concern has been to provide whatever pay and benefit levels appear necessary to attract and retain those individuals with the qualifications required for the jobs to be performed. At the same time a number of companies have given consideration to the motivational aspects of pay policies with a view to designing programs that will induce employees to higher levels of performance. In this sense, compensation policies operate as a mediator in the model of the personnel function in much the same way as development programs do. However, training is directed at *changing* people to make them capable of more effective performance; while pay policies should be designed to motivate employees to use their *existing* capabilities most effectively.

Before discussing pay policies in relation to the motivation of individual employees, we will describe various types of wage and salary programs found frequently in companies today. It should be noted that at the present time management's freedom to change existing practices and even to act within established policies is severely limited by the Federal Government's wage controls program. In general, however, the controls are aimed at keeping down the overall level of increase in wage and salary payments, and they do permit adjustments on an individual basis.

WAGE AND SALARY ADMINISTRATION

A number of activities are carried on in most firms with a view to establishing and maintaining a "sound and equitable" wage and salary program. These activities include procedures for comparing the wage level of the firm with payments made by other companies, for positioning or grading jobs in terms of their relative worth within the firm, and for determining the types of pay systems and supplementary pay practices that are most appropriate for different jobs.

Wage Levels and the Use of Wage Surveys

Over the years, labor economists have studied the wage-level phenomenon from a number of viewpoints. The wage level in individual firms has been related to such factors as skill level, employee satisfaction, profitability, and a multitude of other factors. These studies indicate that a company's wage level is rarely the product of one factor. It does appear, however, that the larger corporations have higher wage levels, and so do those located in highly industrialized and highly unionized communities.

For purposes of the individual company, wages for most jobs will depend on the general wage level in the local area. According to a 1972 survey of BNA's *Personnel Policies Forum*, only for management-level jobs in companies with more than 1,000 employees are competitive wages in the industry a more important factor than area wages in determining wage levels. For the vast majority of companies (97 percent of the PPF firms, for example) data from area or industry wage surveys are used to determine the prevailing wage level. Most companies conduct their own surveys for at least some job categories, and they also rely on survey data from other sources, particularly employer associations and the Bureau of Labor Statistics (BLS) of the U.S. Department of Labor. BLS also is the source of other data often used as criteria for making adjustments in the wage level. These include the monthly Consumer Price Index (CPI), which shows changes in the cost of living nationwide and for various cities throughout the country, and the City Worker's Family Budget, which indicates the income level needed to maintain an adequate standard of living in various cities.

Another criterion for making adjustments in the wage level is the company's financial condition or its "ability to pay" a requested wage increase. Managerial pay levels are likely to be affected to a greater degree when the firm's profit picture is poor, but there are times when even rank-and-file employees represented by a union will forego a wage raise temporarily. In the long run, however, the company's wage level cannot remain too far below the area standard or the more effective employees will be attracted to better-paying jobs elsewhere.

Wage Structures and Job Evaluation

While data from area or industry wage surveys provide a basis for external equity in the pay system, the establishment of a company wage structure based on the relative worth of different jobs is aimed at providing internal equity. Wage surveys make it possible to reduce feelings of inequity when an employee compares his earnings with others outside the firm; an effective wage structure makes it possible to reduce such feelings when internal comparisons are made.

Some companies have relatively simple wage structures with only two or three job classes and one rate for each class; the job structure itself and the pay rates for each job may be determined entirely on the basis of wage surveys. In most organizations, however, the wage structure is far more complex. In order to accommodate the different types and levels of jobs, some companies have as many as 50 or 60 job classes, or pay grades. Nearly all wage structures also involve rate ranges, with a series of steps between the minimum and maximum wage rate for each pay grade. Each step indicates the amount by which an employee's pay will increase when he receives a raise on the same job.

The process for determining the relative ranking of jobs and for deciding which jobs fall into which pay grades is known as *job evaluation*. In many companies this has become an extremely complicated procedure, and outside experts in the field frequently are called in to help set up and to administer the job evaluation system. Various methods are used in job evaluation, but the basic data for all the methods comes from the job description. In some methods the whole job is evaluated on the basis of one factor such as level of decision-making; other methods involve the use of several factors such as skill, mental effort, physical effort, responsibility, and working conditions. Where several factors are used, they may differ for different job categories with the result that there is one job evaluation system applying to factory jobs, another for clerical jobs, a third for sales, and so forth.

For many years job evaluation systems applied primarily to factory jobs; often they were installed because of union complaints about unfair pay practices. In more recent years these systems have been extended to office situations and to lower- and middle-management positions. There also has been some effort at simplifying the job evaluation process because of the difficulty of accommodating new jobs or changes in existing jobs under the more complex procedures. Several studies indicate that evaluation based on one factor is nearly as precise as methods based on several factors. Some companies have turned the job evaluation task over to the employees with the result that the job hierarchy is based on the factors the employees themselves view as relevant and important. This approach is one way of increasing the equity of the wage structure.

Wage Payment Plans

Another variable in the compensation program is whether employees are paid an hourly wage or a weekly or monthly salary. Traditionally, factory jobs have been paid on an hourly basis, while a salary payment is characteristic in the office situation. However, studies have shown that factory employees prefer a weekly salary. Where factory salary plans have been introduced, payroll administration costs have been reduced and there has been no increase in employee absenteeism or tardiness, as was feared.

For casual labor, as in the construction industry, or for any operations where the workweek varies to a large extent, the hourly wage rate is more appropriate. Under more stable conditions, the salary approach seems to offer a number of advantages. Where employees *are* paid on a salary basis, however, it may be necessary to translate the weekly or monthly payment to an hourly rate in order to make comparisons with rates paid in other companies as reported in wage survey data. An hourly rate needs to be determined also for all employees subject to the wage-hour laws for purposes of computing overtime pay.

Supplementary Pay Practices—In addition to the basic hourly or weekly wage, there are a number of supplementary payments that will be reflected in an employee's paycheck. The nature and extent of these payments depend primarily on the type of industry; sometimes they are required by law or specified under a union contract. The most common of these payments is for overtime, usually at the rate of time and one-half the regular hourly rate for hours over eight per day or 40 per week. Under certain circumstances, if the work extends beyond 10 hours in any one day, for example, the overtime rate may go up to double or triple time. Double- or triple-time pay often is required for work on Sunday, work on the sixth or seventh consecutive day of the week, and work on holidays.

Other types of supplementary pay practices, which are found most commonly in manufacturing operations, include *shift differentials*, providing a higher rate of pay for work on the evening or night shift; *reporting pay*, which guarantees a minimum payment, usually of four hours' work, when employees report for work as scheduled and none is available; *call-in pay*, also a guarantee of a minimum payment for employees called in to work at a time when they are not regularly scheduled; and *premium pay* for working under hazardous or undesirable conditions.

Incentive and Bonus Systems—One type of wage payment plan provides for earnings that are directly related to the employee's output or contribution to profits rather than merely to the amount of time spent on the job. There are individual incentive plans, plans based on performance of an entire work group, and plans based on the results of the company as a whole. The latter often take the form of a profit-sharing plan paying an annual bonus.

The most common type of individual incentive is the piece rate, which is based on a measurement of what is considered normal or standard production on a given job. Piece-rate plans date back to the Scientific Management era at the beginning of the century, and they are found primarily in manufacturing operations; they are most effective for routine, repetitive jobs. In recent years, many of these types of jobs have been eliminated by automation, and the individual incentive systems have disappeared or have evolved into group incentives. Group incentive systems are similar to those of an individual nature in that the output of the group is compared with a predetermined standard; however, the earnings are paid from a pool, either in equal shares to all members of the group or in proportion to job level.

Some companies have an incentive pay plan that covers an entire manufacturing operation. An example is the Scanlon plan, which calls for the payment of monthly and year-end bonuses based on savings in labor costs. The Scanlon plan also incorporates an incentive for employees to make suggestions for increased efficiency. This approach has been effective in motivating employees to higher levels of productivity, but it has been used almost entirely in relatively small companies with fewer than 1,000 employees.

Profit-sharing plans usually pay annual bonuses based on the company's profit level for the previous year's operation; unless a certain percentage of profit is attained, no bonus is paid. Such plans are considered a type of incentive system, but they rarely operate as an incentive for nonmanagerial employees, who have little if any control over the production process. For this reason, many firms pay bonuses based on overall company performance only to the managers in charge.

Pay Practices for Management Personnel

Except for the bonus payments just mentioned, most of the wage payment practices discussed so far relate primarily to employees below managerial rank. For a number of reasons the management group usually is treated separately for compensation purposes.

Historically, a major reason for the difference in pay policies is that most supervisors and managers are exempt from the overtime and other requirements of the wage-hour laws. This presents a problem in companies where considerable overtime is worked, especially if highly paid skilled workers are involved; the supervisor may end up with less pay than his subordinates. Most companies try to set the supervisor's salary 10 to 25 percent above his highest paid subordinate, but where overtime or shift work is involved they may also pay an extra premium to maintain this differential. In general, pay practices for the first level of supervision are closely related to the pay of their subordinates, and under some types of incentive plans the supervisors' earnings are based entirely on the earnings of the work group.

At the middle and top levels of management, other factors assume more importance. For large companies that recruit for managers on a national level and for positions requiring special skills or professional training, the salaries paid may be determined entirely on the basis of the state of the labor market and have very little relationship to the company's wage levels for low-level jobs. As one moves up the hierarchy to the top executive, income-tax considerations become a prime concern. A number of approaches have been developed to offset the tax liability of the high income levels— these include deferred payment of profit-sharing bonuses and various forms of stock purchase or stock option plans. A few firms have adopted what is called a "cafeteria" or "smorgasbord" approach to executive compensation in which the individual is permitted to select his own pay package from several alternatives. The choice may involve cash payment, deferred payment, stock plans, and payments for such benefits as life insurance, annuities, or retirement pay. This type of pay plan can be effective in accommodating the differing income needs among top-level executives because of differences in age, family status, and other sources of income.

PAY POLICIES AND EMPLOYEE MOTIVATION

The question of how compensation policies can operate most effectively to motivate employees has only recently been of major interest to behavioral scientists. Most of the procedures we have discussed under the heading "Wage and Salary Administration" are practices relating to entire groups or levels of employees. They are aimed at providing an equitable wage structure from beginning jobs to top management at whatever level is necessary to attract the people needed to fill the jobs available.

Once individuals become employees, pay policies become a different matter. If the compensation program is not administered effectively, employees may feel that their work effort has little or no relationship to their pay, or that others with whom they typically compare themselves either inside or outside the organization are being paid better. Pay policies then become a source of dissatisfaction that can be reflected in poor job performance or eventually in the employee's leaving for a job elsewhere. This type of dissatisfaction may be alleviated by the use of wage surveys, job evaluation systems, or the installation of a wage incentive plan. To turn pay policies from a dissatisfier to a motivator, however, requires that in some way the policies influence individual employees to higher levels of peformance. This usually is a matter of individual wage progression, or the way in which the employee is rewarded periodically for his work effort.

Individual Wage Progression

In recent years a number of theories have been advanced to explain how an individual employee or manager can be motivated by pay. Some of these theories are called *expectancy theories:* they are based on the premises that individuals have certain expectancies regarding the consequences of their own behavior, that they have certain motives or desired outcomes, and that they will behave in a manner that will achieve the desired outcome. Another type of pay motivation theory is *equity theory*, which emphasizes the employee's perception of the fairness of his pay in comparison with that of others doing the same work. Research that has been undertaken to test both types of motivation theories appears to indicate that for job performance to be affected positively by pay policies, employees must perceive that better performance will result in higher pay, they must believe that it is possible to achieve better performance through their own efforts, and they must perceive that their rewards are equitable when compared to the performance and pay levels of their fellow employees.

Unfortunately, the way in which individual wage progression is handled in a majority of companies does not meet these conditions, and the motivational potential of pay is often lost. Outside pressures may well be to blame for this situation. In much of American industry, employees have come to expect yearly wage increases as a result of union bargaining; they get these raises no matter what the quality of their job performance. Nonunion firms also tend to give general across-the-board increases to all employees in times of rising living costs or when wage survey data indicate a need to raise the company wage level to remain competitive in the labor market. Again, wage increases are given irrespective of work behavior.

The approach to individual wage progression that should have a positive impact on job performance is the "merit" plan providing for pay increases based on past performance. With respect to the wage structure, the establishment of rate ranges and steps within the ranges for each job class is done to specify the amount of increase an employee can expect to receive at periodic intervals if his performance is satisfactory. Often, however, employees are given these increases automatically on the basis of seniority rather than on the basis of merit. Just as in the case of general wage increases, employees come to expect a yearly "merit" increase regardless of their performance.

An effective merit pay system is one based on some type of performance appraisal program of the kind discussed in Chapter 5. However, one survey shows that less than half the nation's largest industrial firms have formal systems for evaluating performance even though they indicate that job performance is the primary determinant of progression through the rate range. Even where a formal appraisal program has been introduced, there often are problems in administering it. The major factor is the role of the supervisor, who may be reluctant to deny a pay raise because of poor performance and who may find it extremely difficult to communicate with employees regarding poor performance. This problem is amplified by the differences between supervisors in their approach; one may be a "good guy" and recommend every one of his subordinates for a raise, while another may try to achieve the aims of the merit program and recommend only those whose performance is outstanding. The end result may be that the administration of the merit increase system in different departments is viewed as inequitable.

The Secrecy Issue

One viewpoint advanced by a number of behavioral scientists is that if there were less secrecy surrounding pay policies employees would be more likely to see a relationship between performance and pay. The argument is that if pay procedures, pay rates, and actions taken in wage and salary matters were made public, at least within the company, this would increase the motivational impact of pay.

Except in government employment, where salaries are legislated and a matter of public record, it is true that wage and salary matters usually are treated as confidential information. According to a 1972 BNA survey, managers in more than half the companies represented on the *Personnel Policies Forum* do not have access to salary schedules applying to their own management level, and in less than one fifth do managers generally have any knowledge of the salaries of other managers at their own or higher levels. Even below the management levels, there is a good bit of secrecy. In more than one quarter of the *PPF* companies, rank-and-file employees are not given copies of wage schedules applying to their own job categories, nor are they informed of where this information is available. In nearly two thirds of the companies, employees do not have access to information on wage schedules applying to job categories other than their own. In many instances, where information on wage rates is available, it is limited to jobs covered by a union contract, and employees not represented by the union are not given this information.

Comments from several of the *PPF* members indicate that their companies are moving toward more openness in their pay policies and practices but that there are some problems. One is the difficulty mentioned before of the different values and standards of the supervisors in appraising employee performance. Unless the pay system really is equitable and superior performance is in fact rewarded with higher pay, an open approach may do more harm than good. In such a situation, however, pay obviously is not an effective motivator.

It is clear from a number of studies that the more employees believe that performance influences pay, the harder they will work to improve their performance. On the other hand, it also has become apparent that not all individuals view pay as a primary source of satisfaction. In terms of the motives in Maslow's need hierarchy described in Chapter 6, for example, pay is most closely associated with the satisfaction of physiological and security needs and the ego needs of outside status, esteem, and recognition. Pay policies, then, can be expected to have the greatest impact on the performance of those employees with the greatest need for money *per se* and those employees with a high need for the status and esteem that money represents. Pay is less likely to motivate those employees who are concerned primarily with satisfying social or self-actualization needs, and the question of whether pay policies are secret or open probably has little impact on the performance of such employees.

FRINGE BENEFITS

For the employer, the cost of compensating employees for work performed is not limited to wages and salaries. An increasingly large percentage of payroll costs is in the form of various so-called fringe benefits. According to a U.S. Chamber of Commerce survey, average company payments for employee benefits amounted to 30.8 percent of payroll in 1971, or $2,544 per year per employee.

Some forms of employee benefits go back to the beginnings of industrialization, and a number of large corporations adopted pension and welfare plans during the paternalistic days of the 1920s. It was not until the late 1940s and 1950s, however, that most benefits became firmly established throughout industry. The major impetus came from governmental policies during World War II and Korea providing for wage controls and for taxing excess profits. Employers were discouraged from raising wages but could provide more liberal benefits, and they were encouraged to set up employee benefit plans with funds that otherwise would merely go to pay taxes. The unions soon began to include benefit programs in their lists of bargaining demands, and once the NLRB ruled (in 1948) that companies do have to bargain on such matters, the incidence and coverage of such plans witnessed a dramatic increase.

At the present time, nearly every company offers a myriad of benefits for its employees. The major ones, such as vacations, insurance, and retirement pay, often are described in recruiting literature as a lure to prospective employees. In contrast to actual wages or salaries, however, benefit programs rarely have much impact in recruiting, nor do they have much potential as a motivator in terms of employee performance and productivity. The presence of certain benefits—vacations and holidays, for example—can be expected to contribute to employee morale and general job satisfaction. Other benefits, such as medical insurance and pensions, may help employees satisfy their security needs and thus also contribute to overall job satisfaction. In terms of the organizational goals discussed in Chapter 1, wage and salary programs are more likely to foster the productivity goal, while benefit programs relate primarily to the organizational maintenance goal.

Time-Off Benefits

One group of employee benefits is designed to provide employees certain amounts of time off without loss of pay or loss of job security. These benefits include paid holidays, vacations, and various types of leaves.

Paid holidays, at least six per year, are provided by virtually all companies; in 40 percent of companies there are 10 or more paid holidays. Recently the trend has been to group holidays in clusters around weekends rather than extending the number of isolated holidays. Often this is accomplished by a "floating" holiday which may be observed on a different day each year. In a year in which Christmas falls on a Tuesday, for example, the day before could be designated as the floating holiday.

Paid vacations usually vary from two to five weeks in length, with the longer vacations for the employees with the longest service with the company. Over the years vacation provisions have been liberalized both in the number of weeks off and in the length of service required; in 1960 the maximum vacation specified in a group of union contracts was four weeks, usually after 20 years' service, but by 1970 the maximum was more than six weeks and in some instances employees were eligible for four weeks after ten or 15 years' service. In the steel industry, employees are eligible for extended vacations, or sabbaticals, once every five years. These call for an extra 10 weeks' vacation in addition to the employee's regular three or four weeks. To provide for vacations in industries like construction where employees may work for several different employers over the year, the employer association or union often sets up a vacation fund. Benefits from the fund are based on the number of hours the employee worked during the year.

Paid leave for personal reasons including illness or death in the family is granted to employees in many companies; however, this practice applies more frequently to office and managerial personnel than to factory workers. Other forms of paid leave include time off to vote, which is required by law in some states, and time for jury or other civic duty. In the latter instance, employees usually are paid the difference between the jury-duty pay and their regular pay.

Unpaid leaves of absence may be permitted for a variety of reasons with the advantage to the employee that he can be away from his job for an extended period without losing his job rights and certain benefits that are based on length of service. The most common leaves of absence are for maternity, military service, or education, or to accept a political or union office.

Cash Payments

Another type of benefit program includes payments made under state or federal law and supported by payroll taxes on either the employer or the employer and employee together. These provide benefits for retired employees and medical care for the elderly under the Social Security Act, payments to employees laid off or separated through no fault of their own under the unemployment compensation (UC) system, payments to employees disabled as a result of an on-the-job accident, and to families of employees killed in industrial accidents under the state workmen's compensation (WC) laws, and in a few states benefits for time lost because of illness or injury under temporary disability laws.

Most employers supplement the public benefits, especially those paid under Social Security, and some employers, particularly those in the automobile industry, supplement the state unemployment compensation benefits. These payments are made from supplemental unemployment benefit (SUB) plans negotiated with the union. In some industries it is common to find benefits such as severance or separation pay, retraining allowances, or technological adjustment pay to maintain income of separated employees until they find new jobs.

Other types of cash benefits include year-end or Christmas bonuses, which may or may not be related to profits; savings or thrift plans, in which part or all of the company payment may be in the form of stock; and bonuses paid in recognition of long service or good attendance, or as awards in employee contests or suggestion systems. Because these latter types of payments are not related to public policy and rarely are of major concern to unions, they are not as widespread as the other cash benefits.

Group Insurance

Over the past 30 years, some form of group insurance coverage has been put into effect or made available to nearly all American workers. Even the smallest firms are able to offer such programs through employer associations or other groups. The types of insurance provided are life, sickness and accident, and medical, covering hospitalization and sometimes including major medical expense coverage. Whether or not the company pays the costs of the insurance premiums, these programs are extremely valuable to employees because the group coverage usually is available at far less cost than it would be on an individual basis.

One problem for the personnel department is to determine which of the hundreds of insurance plans available is most appropriate for a particular employee group. A major variable is the cost; if employees are to contribute part of the cost they tend to become quite displeased with a plan that requires a large deduction from their paychecks. Increasingly, however, employers are taking over the entire cost of insurance coverage, and sometimes they even pay for dependent coverage as well. A number of companies have adopted the approach of paying the premium costs for specified basic levels of insurance and making additional benefits available on a contributory basis.

Pensions and Retirement

Like group insurance, pension plans providing payments to supplement the federal Social Security program have become widespread since the union pressures for such programs began in the late 1940s. These plans pay a monthly benefit, the amount of which usually is related to the number of years on the company payroll, upon retirement at age 65, or sometimes age 62. Most plans also make provision for early retirement in the case of permanent disability, and in some companies early retirement is permitted for reasons other than disability.

The tax and other legal aspects of pension plan financing are extremely complex, and most companies rely on financial executives or outside consultants to establish and administer the pension fund. For the personnel department, the important questions with respect to these programs concern such things as whether or not there should be a compulsory retirement age. A compulsory retirement policy may result in all employees being treated equally, but from the company's viewpoint there often are advantages to being able to keep certain employees longer. Furthermore, there is increasing public concern about the status of older people in society, and even the most liberal pension benefits do not equal what an employee would earn if he stayed on the job.

Another matter of public concern regarding pensions is that of the *vesting* of rights to employee benefit payments. Under most pension plans, an employee has to work for the same company for 10 to 15 years before he attains a full right to benefits based on the employer's contribution to the pension fund. Most private pension plans are based on the assumption that employees spend their entire career with one company, but this appears to be less and less the case. Not only do employees change companies, but sometimes a company goes out of business completely; then there is the problem of how to continue paying pensions to employees already retired from the company. These are some of the issues that have led to a number of proposals before Congress to require additional federal regulation of the private pension system.

Public concern of a different kind is confronting personnel management with a major dilemma. Both insurance and retirement benefits increasingly are being viewed as social obligations; employers are expected not only to pay employees adequate wages but also to provide protection in case of illness or layoff and to assure an income for old age. Most of American industry has succeeded in doing this, with the result that employees with steady jobs in large companies have all their security needs taken care of. On the other hand, the hard-core unemployed and people who move frequently from company to company have to rely on public sources. As the private employers provide higher and higher levels of benefits, the disparity between the two groups becomes greater and the public pressure for legislation to provide sizable benefits for all increases.

Administering the Benefit Program

A number of writers have described the situation with respect to employee benefit programs as chaotic. Under pressure from unions or out of a desire to be viewed as progressive employers, companies have set up benefit programs that may make little sense for their particular employees. In many cases there is no attempt to try to analyze the contribution to employee job satisfaction in relation to the costs of providing certain benefits. A bank that did analyze its benefit costs found that nearly half of all the benefit expenses were for post-employment benefits that only those no longer employed would receive.

The actual processing of the paperwork associated with various benefits—requests for leaves, insurance claims, and so forth—answering employee inquiries, and handling complaints regarding benefits is a time-consuming process in most personnel offices. In large organizations there may be the problem of different departments or divisions administering a particular program in conflicting ways.

The crucial factor in the administration of employee benefit programs is the matter of communication. This is true in instances where employees have a choice of benefits and where there are time limits for applying for certain benefits or for filing claims. It also is imperative that supervisors be kept informed about all aspects of the benefit program so that employees are provided accurate information. For the company to realize as much gain as possible from the costs of the benefit program, employees should know what the benefits are and how they work. Several studies show that many employees have no idea what benefits the company pays for. The matter of employee communication programs, as they apply to benefits and all other aspects of employee relations, will be discussed in the next chapter.

Chapter 8

Employee Relations and Communications

The personnel activities described in this chapter differ in a number of respects from those discussed previously. In contrast to the programs for recruiting, selecting, training, and compensating employees, which are found in all companies, formal programs for improving employee relations and communications are nonexistent in many firms. For the most part, it is the larger and longer established company that undertakes this type of effort. Another difference is that there is much greater variability in these activities. There are no legal constraints, except those relating to safety and health, and very little union pressure influencing these programs; thus, the employer is free to provide certain services or not and to take any approach that seems likely to achieve the goal he has in mind. Finally, the objectives of these programs differ in that they do not relate to improving productivity directly, as do most training and wage and salary programs. They are aimed primarily at improving performance by increasing job satisfaction. The goal is to have employees view the company as "a good place to work," not just as a place where they happen to have a job.

As noted in Chapter 2, the question of the relationship between job satisfaction, or the broader concept of employee morale, and performance or productivity has been the subject of widespread study by behavioral scientists over the past 30 years. While there do not appear to be any general principles that apply in all situations, the key to the relationship between satisfaction and performance seems to be the motivational makeup of the individual. Aspects of the job situation, such as pay, that serve to motivate one employee to a higher level of performance may have no effect at all on another employee. According to Herzberg's theory of work motivation (see Chapter 6), employees are more likely to be motivated by factors related to recognition, responsibility, and opportunity for advancement than by wages or working conditions. It is clear, however, that there are widespread individual differences in what employees view as satisfying or dissatisfying about their jobs.

Most studies indicate that the crucial element in employee job satisfaction is the supervisor and his relationship with the work group. In many job situations, the supervisor represents the company to his employees, and it is he who has the ultimate responsibility for the productivity of his group. For this reason supervisory training is a continuing major effort in many companies. It also is for this reason that most measures of employee morale or satisfaction are analyzed on a departmental or work-group basis to pinpoint specific areas where morale may be a problem.

Measures used to appraise employee job satisfaction include some of the same sources discussed in Chapter 5 and used for appraising performance, such as turnover figures, absenteeism rates, and frequency of employee complaints or grievances. In addition, some companies conduct periodic formal attitude surveys or ask supervisors to submit regular reports on the attitudes of their employees. Information from exit interviews when employees leave the company or other types of employee interview programs may also be used as an indicator of morale problems. Another source used in some companies is a study of employee participation rates in company-sponsored activities such as social events, charity drives, contests, or suggestion systems. A careful analysis of all available information may indicate a course of action that could lead to considerable improvement in employee satisfaction and possibly productivity as well. The programs called for may involve procedures for handling individual performance problems, for improving the physical work environment, for providing services that fulfill an employee need or enhance the job, or for establishing a better communications system.

IMPROVING EMPLOYEE PERFORMANCE

An historical premise in personnel research has been that job satisfaction leads to better performance. It has become increasingly apparent, however, that where this correlation does exist there is not a one-way relationship. Good performance on the job can just as well lead to a higher level of job satisfaction, especially if the employee perceives his performance as good and receives some recognition or reward as a result of his performance. The reverse also is true—if an employee feels that he is performing poorly, his morale and job satisfaction are likely to be low.

Recognition of Achievement

Before discussing ways of handling poor performance, we will review the methods used for rewarding good performance. The most obvious form of recognition for a job well done is more money, as a consequence of either a merit increase or a promotion to a better-paying job. In most companies, however, merit increases are limited to one a year with a specified maximum at a certain point, and the number of promotional opportunities decreases as an individual moves up the hierarchy. Because it is not possible to provide a pay increase for every instance of superior performance, many firms have special programs for recognizing outstanding individual achievement. These programs can be expected to be particularly effective in motivating individuals with a high need for self-esteem and the esteem of others.

There is a wide variety of programs of this nature. The rewards may be special bonus payments, certificates or plaques, letters of commendation from company officials, a company-paid vacation trip, or gifts of jewelry or company merchandise. The recognition may be given to professional employees for the publication of scientific or technical articles, to scientific employees who have patents issued or applications for patents filed, or to employees who achieve a certain level of quality workmanship or customer service. The programs often involve contests related to cost or quality control, and some companies have a contest to name an "employee of the year." A common feature of all these programs is that they receive widespread publicity in company publications and sometimes in the local press as well.

Another type of recognition program found in nearly all companies that has been in existence for some time is that of providing awards for service. These awards are mostly of a non-cash variety such as service pins, watches, and certificates, although some companies do give cash bonuses or company stock. These programs also receive extensive publicity. Personnel executives indicate that while this type of program may have little effect on employee performance, the recognition of long-service employees does help to improve employee morale and inspire loyalty to the company.

Procedures for Handling Poor Performance

One of the supervisor's major responsibilities is to appraise his employees' performance both formally at regular intervals and informally on a continuing basis. In instances where an individual employee's performance is not satisfactory, it usually is the supervisor who must take some action to correct the situation. Depending on the resources available, the supervisor may make a recommendation himself or he may call on the personnel department for assistance.

The first step in maintaining performance control is to establish certain standards of minimum acceptable performance. These standards may relate to such matters as extent of absence from work and violation of company rules as well as to an employee's quantity and quality of output. Whenever an employee's behavior falls below these standards, there is an indication that some type of corrective procedure is needed. Exactly what procedure is called for depends on what factors seem to be causing the poor performance; determining the causal factors is the most difficult part of the performance control process. Studies indicate that there are dozens of factors that may contribute to job failure—some of these are factors within the individual, some relate to the organization or groups at work, some stem from family situations, and some are the result of environmental, social, or economic forces. In most cases, more than one factor is involved, and it may take an extended analysis and more than one corrective technique to achieve satisfactory performance. The following discussion covers some of the common causes of poor performance and the most appropriate corrective procedures.

The Job Itself—In many instances, an employee fails to achieve acceptable performance because of factors related to the job itself. An employee may be placed in a job for which he lacks the necessary intelligence or some other ability, or he may not have been given adequate training. Additional training or transfer, perhaps involving a demotion, to a job for which he is qualified may be called for. Transfer also is an appropriate procedure when there are problems of a poor relationship or personality conflict between the employee and his superior or between the employee and others in the work group.

Sometimes an employee has the necessary training and ability, but seems to lack motivation to perform a particular job effectively. One solution here is to find a more challenging job, which may involve promotion. Often, however, there are no vacancies in higher level positions, and an appropriate procedure would be some type of job redesign such as the job-enlargement or job-enrichment approaches discussed in Chapter 4.

Discipline and Discharge—Formal disciplinary action as a procedure for improving performance usually is reserved for situations where the poor performance is related to a violation of company rules dealing with absence from work, insubordination, disorderly conduct, and the like. Such actions often are in the form of a written warning for a first offense, then later a suspension or disciplinary layoff without pay, with discharge as the ultimate step for successive violations. Because of societal pressures, and pressures from the union where one exists, discharge for poor performance occurs only as a last resort. Most companies try to find some corrective action to help employees improve their performance, especially where longtime employees are involved.

Employee Counseling Programs—In cases where poor performance stems from an employee's personal problems—financial, emotional, marital—some type of counseling can be helpful. Many large companies have trained counselors in the personnel department, and employees are encouraged to discuss both job-based and personal difficulties that may be affecting their work behavior. In smaller companies, the personnel manager may take on the counseling function, or supervisors may be given special training in counseling. Many companies work closely with community agencies in referring employees who need outside help.

A major problem in industry today is poor performance resulting from alcoholism. Some companies have their own facilities for the treatment of alcoholics; others maintain a close association with the local chapter of Alcoholic Anonymous to assist their employees with this problem. A more recent, and not yet so widespread, problem is that of drug abuse. A number of companies have established programs relating to the use of drugs with particular emphasis on training supervisors in detecting and helping employees with a drug problem.

THE WORK ENVIRONMENT

One of the earliest studies of employee productivity—the Hawthorne experiment—was designed originally to measure the impact
of changes in physical working conditions such as heat and ventilation on job performance. The major finding was that changes in the
physical environment had less effect on performance than did group
relationships. The physical conditions of the work place may not be
the most important factor in employee performance, but they obviously do affect how employees feel about their jobs. For this reason
most employers take steps to provide as pleasant, clean, safe, and secure a work environment as possible.

Company or outside engineers usually are called in to help with
problems of heating and air conditioning, dust and noise control,
and lighting. In the areas of cleanliness and housekeeping, employee
involvement often is encouraged through contests, clean-up campaigns, and special awards in recognition of good housekeeping. In
manufacturing operations, a major effort with respect to the work
environment concerns safety.

Safety Management

In Chapter 3 we discussed the evolution of industrial safety programs as influenced by the state workmen's compensation laws
enacted in the early 1900s and the more recent federal Occupational
Safety and Health Act. While this legislation has had an impact as far
as company safety programs are concerned, many employers undoubtedly would undertake efforts to minimize hazards in the workplace even in the absence of legal requirements. It is difficult to recruit employees for a job environment that is known to be
dangerous, and performance is likely to suffer when employees are
anxious about real or imagined hazards. Just as it is impossible to
eliminate all potential hazards in the home, so also it is impossible for
an employer to make the work environment absolutely safe. The
goal of the company safety effort is to reduce the danger factor to a
minimum.

To supervise the safety program, most manufacturing companies
designate a specialist in the field who usually works within the personnel department but often has direct authority to stop hazardous
operations. Committees also are used in a majority of companies to
further the safety effort and to encourage employee involvement.

The safety committee may be a joint union-management group, or in nonunionized plants may include employee representatives selected by the supervisors in each department. Committees often are charged with the responsibility for establishing safety rules and penalties for violations, including procedures for handling situations in which employees feel an assignment is too dangerous to be performed. Other activities that are carried out by the safety director and/or the safety committee include the following:

Measuring Safety Performance—Records and reports of on-the-job injuries or accidents are a major ingredient of the safety program. Some accident records and reports are required by state and federal law and for processing insurance claims. The records can be used to compute injury frequency and severity rates, which may be compared with those published by the National Safety Council or by BLS. The accident rates also can be compared between departments or work groups and over different periods of time to indicate where additional efforts may be needed in promoting safety.

Controlling Hazards—A number of steps can be taken to eliminate hazards wherever possible and to minimize those hazards that cannot be eliminated entirely. A job analysis can be made from a safety point of view with the job description indicating how to perform the job in the safest way possible, including the use of protective equipment such as safety shoes, helmets, and goggles. Machinery can be placed so as to provide barriers to exposure to danger, and can be equipped with automatic shut-off devices; especially hazardous areas can be identified with specified colors. An essential aspect of the hazard-control program is a periodic inspection to make sure that all the safety devices are working properly and that employees are following the safety procedures.

Training and Publicity—Both employee and supervisory training programs may include special emphasis on safety. This is particularly important in training new employees since a large percentage of accidents involve inexperienced workers. To maintain a continuing high level of safety consciousness among employees, most manufacturing firms carry on extensive publicity campaigns. Safety promotion contests of various kinds and periodic awards for good safety performance records are common, and many firms make use of posters, booklets and other printed material from the National Safety Council or from insurance companies to increase safety consciousness.

Industrial Security—One aspect of the safety program that has taken on increasing importance as a result of the rash of bomb threats and similar incidents in the late 1960s is the area of industrial security. The concern here is not confined primarily to manufacturing plants as most safety problems are; offices of banks, utility companies, universities, and government agencies and all types of transportation facilities have been threatened. According to a 1972 BNA-ASPA survey, special procedures relating to plant or office security are now found in two thirds of all companies. The effect on employee morale in a situation where there is the possibility of such a threat can be expected to be the same as in any other dangerous situation—employees will be more satisfied with their jobs if they know the company is doing all it can to minimize the danger.

Company Medical Programs

The growth of industrial medicine closely parallels the development of industrial safety. The earliest company medical programs were set up to provide prompt treatment in cases of on-the-job accidents, and this type of first aid and emergency care still is an important part of in-plant medical activities. Companies also use their own medical departments to conduct preemployment physical examinations, to determine when employees are ready to return to work after an illness or injury, and to provide periodic physical examinations, particularly for executives.

Another responsibility of company medical personnel in some industries involves preventive measures with regard to chemicals, gases, fumes, or other noxious elements and with regard to radiation hazards. Industrial physicians and hygienists often are in charge of monitoring the work area and may recommend shutting down an operation or modifying the situation where employee health is endangered.

Because of the large expense involved in maintaining an in-plant medical staff, such a department is found mostly in large companies or in operations that are located in remote areas where no other medical facilities are available. In the latter case, the employer often provides medical care for employees' families as well. In small companies, the medical facilities may be limited to a first-aid dispensary, sometimes with a nurse in charge or with a local doctor on call. Some small firms also employ doctors on a part-time retainer or fee basis to conduct preemployment or periodic physical examinations.

SERVICES FOR EMPLOYEES

In addition to the medical services discussed above, a number of other services for employees are made available in many companies. Some of these are offered in connection with the employee counseling programs mentioned earlier in this chapter. Some services are a function of company location, others relate to type of industry; some are provided because they are unavailable in the community, others because the company can provide the service at far less cost than the cost to an individual employee. The most prevalent types of employee services include the following:

Food Services—These range from one or two vending machines to a full-scale employee cafeteria or an executive dining-room. Nearly all employers provide at least a lunch room or other area where employees can take a break and eat their lunch away from the work location.

Transportation Services—Employees required to travel in connection with their jobs usually are provided assistance in the form of use of company cars or airplanes and reimbursement for expenses as well as help in making travel arrangements and reservations. Company travel bureaus sometimes also help with employees' vacation plans. Other transportation services of concern to employees include parking facilities and assistance with car-pool arrangements.

Housing Services—Company-owned housing is mostly a thing of the past except in remote places where little else is available. When employees are transferred or hired from another location, however, most companies do assist in the move. In addition to the payment of moving expenses, some employers help with sale of the former home and purchase of a new one.

Child-Care Services—With the growing number of mothers employed on a regular basis, a number of companies have undertaken programs for providing day care for children. The facilities sometimes are in the same building where the mothers work; if not they usually are close by. The company may subsidize the entire program, or there may be a fee per child which is less than the mother would have to pay elsewhere.

Recreation and Social Services—An endless variety of programs fall under this heading, including sponsorship of athletic teams and bowling leagues, company parties and picnics, activity groups, travel clubs, ticket bureaus for local theater and other cultural events, and so forth. Some large companies have built special recreation areas with lakes, golf courses, club houses, and camping facilities for employees and their families to use.

Company social activities often are held in conjunction with recognition programs; a common feature of annual company dinners or parties is the presentation of service or other awards to employees. Community service also may be closely tied to the company social program; service clubs may provide employees an opportunity to participate in activities for helping the poor, underprivileged, disadvantaged, or disabled people in the local area.

Educational Services—In addition to the adult-education, tuition-aid, and other self-development programs for employees described in Chapter 6, many companies offer scholarships or educational loans for employees or for their children. Some companies also maintain libraries for employee use; the libraries may include books and periodicals of general interest or may be confined to those related to the business.

Financial and Legal Services—Some companies limit their involvement in employee financial or legal matters to counseling and referral to outside sources of assistance. However, many employers make facilities available for credit unions, which can help meet employees' financial needs without the company's becoming involved. A few companies provide emergency loans or other financial aid under certain circumstances.

Legal assistance and advice concerning such matters as income-tax problems, wage garnishments, and property transfers may be offered by the company legal department or by attorneys retained by the company. Although a few companies provide counseling on any legal matter, in most instances advice is limited to financial questions.

Miscellaneous Services—Employees often are provided services related to the type of business. Manufacturers of consumer goods let employees purchase their products at a discount, banks offer free checking accounts, and department stores usually give a substantial discount on employee purchases.

When large numbers of employees are scheduled to be laid off, especially if they are highly skilled technical or professional employees, companies may provide "out-placement" services. These include help with writing up resumés, secretarial assistance, and making contacts with prospective employers in the area or industry.

It is doubtful that any one company provides all of the possible types of services for employees listed here; on the other hand, many companies do spend a large amount of time and money providing such services. Some services, such as medical and child-care facilities, can be related directly to reducing absenteeism; others, such as food, transportation, and housing services, may be necessary to recruit and retain employees of the caliber the company desires. Most of the other services are provided to encourage employee identification with the company and to improve employee morale. To the extent they are services that some or all of a company's employees want or need, these programs can be expected to contribute to increased job satisfaction.

EMPLOYEE COMMUNICATIONS

An organization's communication system relates to all aspects of the operation, not just to personnel management. There has to be some means of communication for employees and their supervisors to know what work they are expected to perform and how, and there has to be some method for providing management with the information necessary to make decisions for the future.

The basic ingredient of the organizational communication system is the day-to-day, face-to-face interaction between superior and subordinate. This is how jobs are assigned and progress is reported. Because such communication is vital in relation to employee performance, supervisory training and management development programs usually include such topics as communication skills and barriers to effective communication.

In addition to the job-related communication between employees and supervisors, most organizations have some kind of formal communication program designed to keep employees informed about company developments and to provide a means for employees to transmit their ideas, questions, or complaints to management.

These formal communication techniques can contribute to improved job satisfaction to the extent that employees view them as sources of accurate and meaningful information and to the extent there is opportunity for feedback. This is one area where the organizational climate is crucial. The personnel department can set up an elaborate employee-communication system in terms of oral and written media, but it will not be effective if top management is loath to share important information about the company or to take the time and effort to listen to its employees.

The effectiveness of many personnel policies will depend on how good the communication system is. A promotion-from-within policy is not likely to succeed unless employees are kept informed about job vacancies, and the value of many fringe benefits and employee services is lost if employees are not aware of their existence. The communication process is particularly important when new personnel practices are introduced or changes are made in existing policies or practices.

Downward Communication

Studies of the effectiveness of employee communication programs have indicated that the most effective approach to transmitting information from the higher levels of an organization down is a combination of oral and written, formal and informal techniques. This is one reason that such a variety of formal techniques have been developed for downward communication purposes.

Among the written media for employee communications, the most frequently used are weekly, biweekly, or monthly magazines or newspapers, often referred to as house organs; employee handbooks and other booklets describing benefit plans or other aspects of personnel policy; bulletin-board notices and posters; letters mailed to employees' homes; memos to all employees at work or to supervisors; pay inserts; and annual reports. Occasionally management uses advertising or news stories in the local newspapers to communicate certain information to both employees and to the general public at the same time. Oral techniques usually involve meetings of some kind, with supervisors' meetings the most frequently used for communication purposes. Meetings of small groups of employees are held on a regular basis in some companies, and mass meetings of all employees occur under some circumstances. Audio-visual techniques, such as slides, film, TV, and videotape, may be used in connection with employee meetings. Public address systems and taped telephone messages can be used to provide up-to-date or emergency information.

The decision regarding which technique to use in a given instance depends primarily on the type of information involved. Employee manuals are good for use as a reference on company background and basic policy, but bulletin-board notices or memos or letters to employees are better for short items of information that need to be transmitted quickly. If the information is complex, printed media will be more effective than oral. Another variable, however, is the nature of the audience, especially the educational level of the employees involved. Analyses of the readability of employee publications consistently indicate that most of them represent difficult reading for employees whose education is limited. As indicated before, for most types of information, the use of both oral and written techniques is the best way to assure that the message is received and understood by all employees.

What information should be communicated and when is in many instances a matter for top management to decide, especially when matters of company finance or information of potential value to competitors is involved. It is generally agreed that employees want to be informed about how the company is doing and its plans for the future, as well as about changes in pay policies, benefits, or working conditions that may affect them more immediately. In recent years companies have included more material of a controversial nature in employee publications. Management's position in a labor-management dispute may be spelled out, or its views on a political or economic problem may be aired. Studies show that as long as the company's view is clearly labeled as such, employees react favorably toward such efforts. If this type of information is provided only in times of crisis, however, it probably will not be received by employees as favorably as it would be if they were used to reading management's viewpoint in company publications on a regular basis.

Upward and Two-Way Communication

In contrast to the variety of techniques for downward communication, methods for sending information up from the lower to the higher levels of the organization are quite limited. One reason for this situation is that in most organizations it is assumed that those at the higher levels should tell employees below them what to do and how to do it. It is important to provide some mechanism for upward communication, however, so that management will know whether employees have received and understood its downward communications. Furthermore, unless there is some provision for employees to ask questions, make suggestions, or register complaints, major problems of morale and dissatisfaction may develop over a period of time to the point of open conflict before management is aware of any difficulty.

As is the case with downward communication, the most frequent exchanges of information are those between superior and subordinate, and most companies encourage supervisors to elicit ideas from the members of their work group. There is no guarantee, however, that when an employee complains or makes a suggestion about some aspect of his work to his supervisor it will go higher. The supervisor may feel that the matter involved reflects poorly on his own performance, or he may consider it too unimportant to bother with. To overcome this problem, there are several techniques companies may use.

Perhaps the most effective upward communication technique is the formal attitude survey; the use of such surveys will be discussed in a separate section at the end of this chapter. Other techniques provide for both upward and downward employee communications. This is true, for example, of employee meetings, particularly those conducted on a small-group basis. In some firms, the company president or a representative from the personnel department meets with small groups of employees to hear their ideas and to answer questions.

A formal complaint or grievance procedure such as those discussed in Chapter 3 is another vehicle for upward communication. An increase in the use of a formal grievance system may reflect a breakdown in employee relations at some point, although in unionized situations it may merely indicate increased militancy on the part of the union leadership. A further source of feedback from employees is the counseling or interviewing program mentioned earlier in connection with handling poor performance. In most counseling programs, however, the specific personal problems of employees are considered confidential, and the counselor rarely transmits such problems to higher management.

Suggestion systems also are viewed as a means for encouraging upward communication as well as for promoting more employee in-

volvement and greater productivity. A formal suggestion plan out-
lines the types of ideas eligible for consideration and the awards,
usually cash, payable for acceptable suggestions. Employee involvement is encouraged further by the use of committees in administering the suggestion system.

Other sources of upward communication include gripe boxes
for employees to register anonymous complaints, information from
union representatives, question-and-answer columns in the employee newspaper, and the informal grapevine, which is considered
the least effective source of all. A number of companies recently
have set up special two-way channels of communication using telephone message systems in which the employee with a question or
problem can dial a special code and leave a recorded message. With
this system the employee can get an answer more quickly than with
the newspaper question-and-answer device. When the telephoned
question is felt to be of general interest, the company's answer can
be communicated in the regular employee publication.

Employee Attitude Surveys

A formal attitude survey is the most direct method of uncovering sources of employee dissatisfaction and areas of company policy where employees are uninformed or misinformed. Some companies conduct attitude surveys only when there is some reason to
believe there are specific problems in employee relations that need
attention or when a union organizing drive is imminent. Because of
the expense and time involved in conducting such surveys, and also
because of union resistance, employee attitude surveys are not conducted on a regular basis in most companies. Among the employers
on BNA's *Personnel Policies Forum*, for example, less than one
fourth use formal attitude surveys to obtain employee opinion about
their jobs and about the company.

Attitude surveys can be conducted on a one-time basis or at periodic intervals; they can include all employees, a random sample of
employees, or only specified work groups; the questions may relate
to all aspects of the work situation, or they may be limited to one or
two areas. Some surveys are made on the basis of interviews, but this
procedure is extremely time-consuming, and the more common approach is to use a written questionnaire. Sometimes the questionnaires are mailed to employees' homes. If the survey is being conducted by an outside consultant or research firm, employees may be

instructed to mail the questionnaire directly to the outside firm. To encourage open and honest responses, employees usually are not asked to identify themselves on the questionnaire.

Although there may be some value in letting employees know management is interested in their opinions by conducting an attitude survey, the real value lies in the action taken based on the results of the survey. In a few companies, the survey results are treated as confidential information for management guidance only, but most companies make some effort to report the results to the employees who participate. Sometimes a detailed summary appears in the employee newspaper. Studies of the feedback process indicate that employee reactions are more positive when survey results are reported to them in meetings conducted by their supervisors and where there is an opportunity for open discussion.

When the survey results point to a specific area of dissatisfaction, it is important to try to determine the causes of the dissatisfaction. In one survey among 400 office workers, one area of dissatisfaction concerned promotion. Further analysis indicated that the problem was not in the company's overall promotion policies but the fact that many of the employees felt they were in "dead-end" jobs with little chance of moving up. The company's solution was to initiate a policy of encouraging transfers to departments with more promotional opportunities.

If the attitude survey identifies a problem that the company is not in a position to solve, the best approach appears to be to provide a frank discussion of the existence of the problem and the reasons for not being able to do anything about it. Employees at the very least may appreciate that management has listened to their complaints.

Used properly, the attitude survey can provide one of the most effective ways of monitoring the entire personnel process. Attitude-survey data are particularly useful with respect to the personnel activities discussed in this chapter—activities that are aimed at increasing employee job satisfaction and company involvement and thus contributing to the goal of organizational maintenance.

This concludes our description of the personnel process as it is carried out in organizations today. We have tried to describe, at least briefly, all the activities that are the responsibility of the typical personnel department and give an indication of how these activities relate to one another in the management of human resources. The final part will explore some of the current problems of the personnel management field and its prospects.

PART III

The Prospects for Personnel Management

Chapter 9

Current Issues
Confronting Personnel Management

Throughout this discussion of the personnel process and of the activities of the personnel staff, we have tried to highlight current ideas and trends, particularly as indicated by research. In this chapter, we will review a number of problems currently facing the personnel practitioner as reported in recent literature and by personnel executives directly. Some of these issues stem from social and economic forces completely outside the realm of management and personnel management; others have evolved from developments within the personnel and management fields. The extent to which any one of these problems influences an organization will vary from one time to another and from one company to another. It may be expected, however, that sooner or later these problems will have some impact on nearly every personnel department.

OUTSIDE PRESSURES

Societal Values and Governmental Influence

Without doubt the most drastic changes that are occurring in the field of personnel management are the result of societal pressures as reflected in governmental action, especially action related to equal opportunity in employment. Employers doing business with the Federal Government probably have been influenced to the greatest extent, but the effects of efforts by the EEOC and the OFCC are being felt throughout the economy. Under prodding from these agencies, traditional personnel practices that have been considered standard operating procedure for decades have been seriously challenged.

In response to charges of discrimination on the basis of race or national origin, companies have rewritten many of their job specifications to eliminate unnecessary educational requirements, and a number have revised their selection procedures to permit the employment of minority-group members. For many jobs the emphasis has shifted from the input processes of recruiting and selection to the mediating process of training and development. With respect to the government's more recent efforts related to sex discrimination, the impact in many firms has been even greater than that related to other types of discrimination. The nation's largest nongovernment employer, the Bell Telephone System, has drastically changed its job and wage structure, which for 40 or 50 years had utilized strictly male plant-job categories and strictly female operator and office categories. Now magazine advertisements for the Bell System often feature male operators and female telephone installers.

In addition to the pressures to provide equal opportunity in employment, there are other aspects of the personnel function which have been influenced by societal values. The whole concept of the employment relationship as involving an obligation on the part of the employer to provide for the employee's welfare whatever the exigency has resulted in large-scale programs of employee benefits and services in many companies. It is likely, however, that more and more of these programs will become subject to governmental regulation in order to extend such benefits to all workers. This already has happened in the area of industrial safety and health; the disparity in the accident rates between companies and industries with heavy emphasis on safety management and those with minimal safety programs was one factor leading to the passage of the 1970 Occupational Safety and Health Act.

Other, long-standing areas of societal and governmental influence on personnel policy, such as union relations and wage and salary administration, continue to present problems. In labor relations a major concern today is with governmental employment and with public educational institutions, hospitals, and so forth, which increasingly are becoming subject to labor relations legislation. With respect to wage and salary policies, the governmental influence is two-fold, and in many instances conflicting. On the other hand, Congress periodically raises the legal minimum wage, causing an upward movement in wage levels generally, while on the other hand, the administration has taken numerous steps to keep wage levels down through direct controls.

Changes in the Workforce

Another type of influence on today's personnel practices involves the changing nature of the work force. In contrast to the working population of even a decade ago, today's work force is younger and better educated, and includes a higher proportion of women. All of these factors have implications for programs in the areas of training and development, employee relations, and communications.

Of even greater importance is the apparent change in the values of the new generation of workers—they do not appear to be motivated in the same way as people who entered the labor market some five or 10 years ago. It may be that the basic needs of the new generation—physiological and safety—have been met, and that they anticipate these needs will continue to be met in the future, with little or no effort on their part. Accordingly, what they look for in the job situation would relate only to their social, ego, or self-actualizing needs. The implication for personnel management is that policies regarding such programs as compensation and employee discipline may well need to be revised if they are to have any impact on employee performance.

Recent college graduates in particular seem to differ from those of a few years earlier in their attitudes toward work, especially work in large business organizations. If tomorrow's managers are to be recruited from today's college graduates, it may be necessary to make changes in the way organizations are structured with a move toward smaller, more autonomous units. This should provide lower level managers with increased responsibility for making their own decisions and more freedom in implementing these decisions.

PROBLEMS WITHIN PERSONNEL MANAGEMENT

One problem that a number of personnel departments have faced is the historically low esteem accorded the personnel manager in many organizations. According to one personnel executive, the old-fashioned personnel man was viewed as a "hack," and one

writer has called the personnel department the "trashcan" department because all the responsibilities no other department wanted
devolved upon it. In a number of companies these responsibilities
were confined to such things as processing paperwork, assigning
parking spaces, and planning the company Christmas party. Unfortunately, in the eyes of some managers, particularly older ones, this
view of personnel management persists. This is one reason that some
companies try to avoid the term "personnel" and have a "manpower" or "human resources" department instead. This problem of
personnel's image is closely related to the following present-day difficulties in the field as well.

Implementing the Results of Behavioral Science Research

It should be obvious from the ideas we have emphasized
throughout this book that we firmly believe in the value of behavioral science research as it applies to personnel management. However, in all honesty we should caution others in the field that ours is
not a universal point of view, particularly outside personnel itself.
Managers, especially those conditioned to looking at things in terms
of immediate dollars and cents figures, often become disturbed at
the mere mention of the words "behavioral science."

In part, this is the fault of certain behavioral scientists themselves. According to a behavioral scientist at Genesco who is quoted
in a Conference Board report, "some of them work fulltime at trying
to convince people that behavioral science concepts are mysterious
and can be understood only by a chosen few." His advice is to avoid
identifying behavioral science concepts as such because this type of
identification tends to hamper efforts to implement them.

Other aspects of the problem of behavioral science research are
that it often takes a long time for the results to become known, and
there is always the possibility that the results may be negative. A
company president is not likely to be pleased with research results
indicating that a management development program costing hundreds of thousands of dollars has had no measurable impact on the
managers' performance. As a consequence, all too often the solution
is to take a program on faith and not even try to find out whether it is
effective.

Another solution has been to introduce a technique or program
on the basis of results in a different organization without fully testing
its effectiveness within the company involved. This approach has

added to personnel management's negative image; the personnel manager is viewed as "technique-happy," or as always on the look-out for a new "gimmick" to improve employee relations. "Manage-ment by objectives" and "job enlargement" programs are examples of techniques currently in vogue. While they certainly have achieved positive results in some situations, they do not provide panaceas for all types of employees or all job categories.

The Line-Staff Conflict

One result of the emphasis on behavioral science concepts in some organizations has been to increase the traditional conflict be-tween line managers and the personnel staff, at least initially. It takes considerable persuasion and educational effort to convince a pro-duction foreman to try a new approach in supervising his work group, especially if the results do not appear likely to have any im-mediate, positive effect on productivity. Only if higher management fully supports the program and there is good evidence that it will produce positive results in the long run is the supervisor likely to try it with any enthusiasm.

An even more difficult feature of the relationship between per-sonnel and line management today relates to governmental pres-sures for equal employment opportunities. If supervisors have the fi-nal authority in hiring decisions, it is much more difficult to introduce minority-group members into the work force. The super-visor himself may be strongly biased or more probably he may feel that, because of the prejudices of some members of his work group, he should not introduce someone of a different race or color into the group. Similarly, the supervisor of an all-male work group may feel that the presence of a female might well interfere with getting the job done. To effect the changes in selection decisions needed to achieve compliance with FEP regulations, the personnel staff must have control. However, having such control does not always pro-duce less conflict with line managers.

Evaluating the Effectiveness of Personnel Policies

A problem that always has plagued personnel management is how to measure the effectiveness of its work. The outputs of manu-facturing, finance, sales, or engineering departments are readily quantifiable, and in business organizations the contributions of these departments to the company's profit or loss are clearly visible. This is not true of the contribution of the personnel department, and in small, highly competitive companies this is another factor contributing to the low status of the personnel area.

In some companies the personnel staff sets goals for the year for such tasks as the completion of a job analysis program or the introduction of a new supervisory training program. The department's performance then is evaluated on the basis of how well the goals are met. In many firms the personnel department is viewed as doing a good job as long as employees continue to reject any union overtures or as long as there always is a good supply of suitable job applicants. These measures, however, do not provide any clear indication of the impact of the personnel program on the organization's primary goal, such as producing a product, providing a service, or making a profit.

There are some dollars-and-cents measures that can be related directly to the personnel department's efforts. These include the costs of on-the-job accidents, the amount of time away from work and other expenses of handling grievances and collective bargaining, and costs related to absenteeism and turnover. One problem with the use of turnover figures as a measure of personnel policy effectiveness is that they do not always indicate the quality of the individuals who leave the company. If the people who leave are the poorer performers and they are replaced by better performers, a certain level of turnover may be to the company's benefit, at least in terms of costs. Unless there is a continuing system for appraising employee performance, however, it may be impossible to relate turnover to organizational productivity.

The lack of any system for measuring employee performance or employee attitudes is the greatest obstacle to appraising the work of the personnel department itself in many organizations. Even in companies that do have formal appraisal programs, there are problems of deciding what factors should be used as the criteria for measuring performance and, as discussed in Chapter 5, the difficulty of maintaining similar appraisal standards among the many managers making the appraisals. Attitude-survey data also may present problems, particularly where self-report questionnaires are used. One researcher recently questioned the use of such measures in view of increasing discussion in the press and congressional hearings on the subject of worker alienation and job dissatisfaction. Such publicity might well influence an employee to think he should be dissatisfied with his job, and to answer an attitude questionnaire accordingly, even though he cannot point to any specific aspects of the job causing the dissatisfaction. It appears that another problem for the personnel researcher is to develop more sophisticated measuring instruments for appraising employee performance and satisfaction.

Fortunately for the personnel executive there are current developments that point to ways of resolving some of the issues described here. It is possible that in coping with the pressures from outside the organizational environment, personnel managers may find solutions to some of the long-standing problems of the field within organizations. This possibility is discussed in the final chapter.

CHAPTER 10

The Future of Personnel Management

"I have never had any more fun in my life than I have had work-ing in personnel." This is how a member of BNA's *Personnel Policies Forum* describes his reaction to being a personnel executive today, and by "fun" he is not referring to an office picnic. In fact, as director of personnel services for a large state university, he had spent most of the week in meetings with top-level university officials setting up procedures to encourage the promotion of women into higher posi-tions both on the faculty and in the administrative staff. Without some progress along these lines, the university was threatened with the loss of a major share of its income from federal funds to support educational projects.

Some variant of this situation is occurring daily in organizations throughout the country, business and nonbusiness, large and small. Employers increasingly are being faced with the prospect of loss of income from government contracts or an expensive court action un-less certain personnel policies and practices are changed. Although the possibility of this type of pressure has existed for some time, it in-creased greatly with the Supreme Court's decision in 1971 upholding the EEOC in the Duke Power Company case and the granting of di-rect enforcement powers to the EEOC by congressional action in 1972. While these pressures present many problems for personnel management, they also provide a major challenge that may ulti-mately enhance the field considerably. Here are some of the pros-pects for personnel management that we see as probable devel-opments resulting from the current situation.

Personnel's Increased Visibility and Authority

One immediate result of governmental pressures for equal em-ployment opportunities is the inclusion of the personnel officer in some of the highest policy-making groups in the organization. This is illustrated in the university situation described at the beginning of this chapter; in many companies such a situation may be the first opportunity the personnel executive has had to participate in such top-level activities. In some companies the personnel manager has not been included because of the "trashcan" image noted in Chapter 9. But in many firms the reason for not including personnel people in such deliberations was that the majority of top-level decisions relate directly to long-term production or marketing plans, or to finances. Because the current pressures relating to personnel policies do include financial aspects, the personnel executive has become a vital contributor to the organizational decision-making process. Hundreds of thousands of dollars may be involved in suits brought under the Equal Pay Act and similar legal actions.

In addition to making personnel management more visible in the organization's higher echelons, the outside pressures also can be expected to result in increasing centralization of authority with regard to personnel decisions in such areas as hiring and promotion. As noted in Chapter 9, this development may add to the traditional line-staff conflict over personnel matters. However, it is likely that higher management will tend to support the personnel department more than it has at times in the past when there has been conflict of this type. Over time, these conflicts may be mitigated, especially if line management comes to view the personnel department as having legitimate authority and expertise.

Whether or not personnel management will retain its increased visibility and authority once the outside pressures have lessened is another question. A similar opportunity arose during the 1930s and 1940s when management faced extremely difficult problems with large-scale union organizing drives. In many companies, the personnel department simply did not rise to the occasion, with the result that plant managers, company attorneys, or outside experts were given the responsibility for handling labor relations. Often the labor relations group completely overshadowed the rest of the personnel component, and the personnel manager remained in a low status position.

Such a situation could occur again, but for several reasons this appears to be unlikely. First, one gains the impression that the personnel officer typically is being called on to provide solutions himself; line management is not trying to resolve the issues on its own, but is asking for help from the experts. Second, the personnel department increasingly is in an ideal position to provide the expert assistance necessary.

The Increasing Expertise of Personnel Professionals

In Chapter 2, we traced various developments over the past 25 to 30 years that have contributed to a more professional approach to personnel management. These developments include the formation of a number of professional associations, the introduction of several periodicals in the field, and a tremendous increase in research relating to aspects of the employer-employee relationship. All these activities have resulted in upgrading the field in both the academic and business worlds and in providing individuals with expert knowledge to deal with personnel problems.

Further evidence of the growing professionalization of personnel management is provided by the increasing number of consultants and research firms devoted to personnel activities. Even the most well-educated personnel executive cannot be an expert in all aspects of the field, and except in the nation's largest corporations the expense of maintaining a large staff of experts on a permanent basis is not warranted. Fortunately, there are many qualified consultants available to advise on almost any personnel program in question; often these individuals help get a program established, set up procedures for the company personnel staff to administer the program, and monitor it on a periodic basis.

An important element of the work of many personnel consultants as well as the company personnel staff involves conducting ongoing research on the effectiveness of the programs undertaken. Much of this research has turned out to be crucial in discrimination cases; only the results of this type of research can be used to argue effectively that a particular personnel practice does in fact relate to job performance. And it is this type of research that provides the personnel professional with his expertise; he can rely on data rather than hunches. Increasingly, also, the results of personnel research are being translated into dollars-and-cents savings to management.

The Increasing Importance of Human Resource Management

Aside from all the societal and governmental pressures influencing the growth of personnel management, there is another factor pointing to a larger role for the personnel function in organizations of the future. This relates to the increasing importance of the management of human resources in terms of its contribution to company productivity. Advances in engineering technology have reached the point where it is increasingly difficult to improve productivity to any large extent by devising new machinery. Sizable increases in productivity must come as a result of higher levels of job performance, and the company whose employees are performing at high levels is likely to be in the best competitive position.

The matter of worker productivity on the national level is one of the concerns that led to the government's imposition of wage controls in 1971. Because wage increases were outstripping increases in productivity, the economy was adversely affected. Some economists have suggested that a company's freedom to raise wages and/or prices be tied directly to increased employee productivity. Such a policy certainly would generate additional governmental pressure influencing personnel policies and could stimulate an entirely different emphasis in the field of human resource or personnel management.

One of the challenges in the field is to find ways of measuring performance on jobs where no tangible product or service is involved and relating these measures to overall company productivity. A promising development related to human resource management is that of human-asset accounting, which uses accounting procedures much the same as those that provide a statement of a company's financial position. A periodic human-asset accounting provides a similar type of statement with regard to the company's personnel position. Such an approach could well lead to a solution of the problem of measuring the effectiveness of the company's overall personnel program and its contribution to the achievement of the organization's task goals.

The importance of human resource management also has increased greatly with the changing nature of the work force and with the differing values being brought to the job situation. Some writers suggest that in the not too distant future, employers may have to provide a work environment that entices people to become employees to a much greater extent than they do now. Companies will not just be competing with each other for employees; they will be competing with the individual's option not to work at all; there are numerous indications that the no-work option is increasingly attractive to the younger generation. On the other hand, some of the values of the younger generation may operate to solve personnel problems in certain areas. Recent college graduates coming into management positions often have worked with women in both classroom and outside activities on an equal basis; they can be expected to accept women in positions of authority and responsibility in business more readily than the older manager who views the work situation as strictly a man's world. Similarly, the more humanistic values of many of the younger workers should make it easier to integrate blacks and other minorities into the work force.

Conclusion

As we have tried to demonstrate in this and the preceding chapters, the field of personnel management today is facing unprecedented challenges from within and outside organizational boundaries. In essence, it is in meeting these challenges that the personnel executive may find his own job satisfaction—or "fun" in his work, as our *PPF* member describes it. Those entering the field at the present time have a tremendous opportunity, greater than ever before, to make a major contribution to their organization's effectiveness.

In the long run, the effects of the current pressures from the government, from society in general, and from the younger generation cannot help but contribute to the importance of the role of the personnel executive. And as personnel practice becomes more professional and scientific, the old-fashioned "trashcan" image of the field could easily disappear. Similarly, the traditional conflict between the personnel staff and line supervisors may be minimized or even eliminated as the personnel department increasingly comes up with solutions to problems of human-resource management that work.

Under governmental pressures, many recent changes in personnel practice have occurred very quickly. However, the more fundamental changes—changes in the role of the personnel department and in the organization's overall philosophy of human-resource management—may evolve over a considerably longer period of time. To effect such changes, a great deal more needs to be known about how different personnel policies and practices actually influence an organization. While some types of personnel programs—selection techniques, for example—have been the subject of much behavioral science research over many years, other programs, such as pay policies, have only recently been studied in this way. Because research of this kind is increasing steadily, the answers may be forth-coming more rapidly in the future than they have been in the past.

A basic concern in the current research being done in the field involves attempts to answer questions relating to employee motiva-tion and productivity. Under what circumstances is a particular per-sonnel policy or procedure likely to affect performance? What are he personality or other differences among individuals that deter-mine which ones can be motivated by a particular policy and which ones probably will not be motivated by such a policy? Answers to these and similar questions should go a long way toward solving the riddle of the job satisfaction-motivation-productivity relationship.

It is to be hoped that with the greater emphasis on human-resource management, personnel managers and personnel research-ers will identify approaches that will lead to both increased em-ployee productivity and increased job satisfaction. The result could be a substantial improvement in organizational effectiveness with a corresponding improvement in the quality of life in the world of work as well.

PART IV
Source Material

BNA Surveys

Frequently throughout this book reference is made to various surveys that have been conducted by The Bureau of National Affairs, Inc. There are two types of BNA surveys relating to personnel practice; these are described below with a list of recent survey reports.

Personnel Policies Forum (PPF) Surveys

BNA's *Personnel Policies Forum*, a nationwide panel of personnel executives from organizations of all sizes and in many different industries, has been in existence since 1951. The panel is changed periodically—currently every two years—and at present numbers approximately 300 members. Recent PPF survey reports, which are published in booklet form, include the following:

Recruiting Practices (PPF Survey No. 86), March 1969
Fringe Benefit Practices (PPF Survey No. 87), August 1969
Training Employees (PPF Survey No. 88), November 1969
Executive Compensation (PPF Survey No. 89), December 1969
Absenteeism and Its Control (PPF Survey No. 90), June 1970
Turnover and Job Satisfaction (PPF Survey No. 91), July 1970
The Personnel Department (PPF Survey No. 92), November 1970
Tools of the Personnel Profession (PPF Survey No. 93), March 1971
Community Relations (PPF Survey No. 94), May 1971
Status of First-Level Supervisors (PPF Survey No. 95), November 1971
Women & Minorities in Management and in Personnel Management (PPF Survey No. 96), December 1971
Wage & Salary Administration (PPF Survey No. 97), July 1972

> Allowances for Employee Expenses (PPF Survey No. 98), August 1972
>
> The Employer and Higher Education (PPF Survey No. 99), November 1972
>
> Employee Recognition Programs (PPF Survey No. 100), December 1972

ASPA-BNA Surveys

A joint project of BNA and the American Society for Personnel Administration which began in 1969, these surveys are conducted among a special panel of officers and members of ASPA. The panel is made up of a nation-wide sample of 350 personnel executives from many types of organizations, and the membership is rotated periodically. Survey reports are published as a special supplement to BNA's weekly *Bulletin to Management*. The following list includes all the ASPA-BNA survey reports that have been issued.

> Emergency Shutdowns, March 20, 1969
> Monday Holidays, May 15, 1969
> Wage Garnishment, May 15, 1969
> Employing the Disadvantaged, August 14, 1969
> Management and the Generation Gap, December 11, 1969
> Employment of Women, March 5, 1970
> The Employee and the Community, September 24, 1970
> The Employee with Problems, December 10, 1970
> Use of Consultants, March 4, 1971
> Older & Retired Employees, August 5, 1971
> The Economy & the Personnel Department, May 27, 1971
> Personnel Testing, September 9, 1971
> The Changing Workweek, January 6, 1972
> Industrial Security, March 16, 1972
> Holiday Practices, August 17, 1972
> Manpower Programs, December 14, 1972
> Impact of OSHA on Personnel Management, March 8, 1973

Acronyms Used in the Text

The following acronyms are ones frequently encountered in personnel literature. This list is not intended to be all-inclusive but does include all the acronyms appearing in the text.

AAA—American Arbitration Association

AFL-CIO—American Federation of Labor-Congress of Industrial Organizations

AMA—American Management Association

APA—American Psychological Association

ASPA—American Society for Personnel Administration

BFOQ—Bona Fide Occupational Qualification

BLS—Bureau of Labor Statistics

BNA—The Bureau of National Affairs, Inc.

CPI—Consumer Price Index

DOT—*Dictionary of Occupational Titles*

EEOC-—Equal Employment Opportunity Commission

FEP—Fair Employment Practice

FLSA—Fair Labor Standards Act

FMCS—Federal Mediation & Conciliation Service

GATB—General Aptitude Test Battery

IRRA—Industrial Relations Research Association

JIT—Job Instruction Training

JOBS—Job Opportunities in the Business Sector

MBO—Management by Objectives

MDTA—Manpower Development & Training Act

NAB—National Alliance of Businessmen

NICB—National Industrial Conference Board (shortened to Conference Board in 1970)

NLRB—National Labor Relations Board

OD—Organization Development

OFCC—Office of Federal Contract Compliance

OJT—On-the-Job Training

OSHA—Occupational Safety & Health Act
PPA—Public Personnel Association
PPF—Personnel Policies Forum
SPA—Society for Personnel Administration
SUB—Supplemental Unemployment Benefits
UC—Unemployment Compensation
USES—United States Employment Service
WC—Workmen's Compensation

Suggested References

For the reader who would like to study in detail any of the subjects covered in the text, we offer the following list of references as a starting point. In some instances, the references are basic source material; others represent new or current aspects of the topic discussed.

Chapter 1—Defining Personnel Management

Finley, Robert E. (ed.), *The Personnel Man and His Job*. American Management Association, 1962.
Chapters by 47 executives cover the various aspects of the personnel function.
Janger, Allen R., *Personnel Administration: Changing Scope and Organization*. National Industrial Conference Board, 1966.
A report of the results of a survey on personnel administration in 249 companies.
McFarland, Dalton E., *Company Officers Assess the Personnel Function*, American Management Association Research Study No. 79, 1967.
A survey covering the goals and activities of personnel managers, chief executives, and operating executives.
Miner, John B., "An Input-Output Model for Personnel Strategies: Solving Human Resource Problems," *Business Horizons*, June 1969.
A model of the personnel function with implications for organization structure and strategy.
Miner, John B., and Mary Green Miner, *Personnel and Industrial Relations: A Managerial Approach* (2nd ed.), Macmillan, 1973.
A college textbook for introductory courses in personnel management which contains details relating to the research evidence referred to in this book.

Ritzer, George, and Harrison M. Trice, *An Occupation in Conflict: A Study of the Personnel Manager.* New York State School of Industrial and Labor Relations (Cornell University, Ithaca, N.Y.), 1969.
> Results of a survey based on a questionnaire and in-depth interviews with members of the American Society for Personnel Administration.

Wasmuth, William J., and others, *Human Resources Administration: Problems of Growth and Change.* Houghton Mifflin, 1970.
> Four parts, each of which presents the findings of a research project in a major area of personnel management.

Yoder, Dale, *Personnel Management and Industrial Relations*, Prentice-Hall, 1970.
> Sixth edition of a classic textbook in the field.

Chapter 2—The Evolution of Personnel Management

Eilbert, H., "The Development of Personnel Management in the United States," *Business History Review*, Vol. 33 (1959).
> A basic reference article on the history of personnel management.

George, Claude S., Jr., *The History of Management Thought*, Prentice-Hall, 1972.
> Summary of management thought from prehistoric era to the present.

Korman, Abraham K., *Industrial and Organizational Psychology*, Prentice-Hall, 1971.
> A textbook highlighting the contributions of industrial psychology to personnel management.

Ling, Cyril C., *The Management of Personnel Relations: History and Origins.* Irwin, 1965.
> Detailed history of the development of personnel management in the United States.

Nash, Allan R., and John B. Miner (eds.), *Personnel and Labor Relations: An Evolutionary Approach.* Macmillan, 1973.
> A readings book containing statements and articles dating back to 1900 by such pioneers in the field as Taylor and Gompers.

Ritzer, George, "The Professionals," *Personnel Administrator*, May-June 1971.
> Discussion of professionalism in personnel occupations.

Wren, Daniel A., *The Evolution of Management Thought*. Ronald, 1972.
A comprehensive treatment of the historical development of the field.

Chapter 3—Influences on Personnel Decisions

ASPA-BNA Survey: "Use of Consultants," *Bulletin to Management*, March 4, 1971.
Report indicating areas of personnel management for which consultants are most frequently used and describing employer experience with consultants.

Beal, Edwin F., and E. D. Wickersham, *The Practice of Collective Bargaining*, Irwin, 1967.
Basic text providing detailed treatment of collective bargaining.

Blum, A. A., M. Estey, J. W. Kuhn, W. A. Wildman, and L. Troy, *White-Collar Workers*, Random House, 1971.
Series of essays relating to problems of white collar workers and unionization.

BNA Editorial Staff, *The Civil Rights Act of 1964*, BNA Books, 1964.
A definitive explanation and analysis of the Act and how it is applied.

_____, *The Job Safety and Health Act of 1970*, BNA Books, 1971.
Analysis, legislative history, and text of the Occupational Safety and Health Act of 1970

_____, *Major Labor Law Principles Established by the NLRB and the Courts*, BNA Books, 1973.
Tabular presentation of major labor law decisions from December 1964 to December 1972 with editorial comments on the background and significance of each case.

Byham, William C., *The Uses of Personnel Research*. American Management Association, 1968.
Description of personnel research activities in major companies.

Byham, William C., and Morton E. Spitzer, "Personnel Testing: The Law and Its Implications," *Personnel*, September-October 1971.
Discussion of the effect of FEP legislation and executive orders on company practices.

Cohen, Sanford, *Labor in the United States*, Merrill, 1970.
A comprehensive textbook in labor relations.

Miner, John B., "Bridging the Gulf in Organizational Performance," *Harvard Business Review*, July–August 1968.
Presentation of an approach to organizational analysis based on the assumption that organizations are successful to the degree that efforts of individual members are integrated with its goals.

Simkin, William E., *Mediation and the Dynamics of Collective Bargaining*, BNA Books, 1971.
Analysis of the mediation process with special attention to crisis bargaining and emergency disputes, written by a former director of the Federal Mediation and Conciliation Service.

Updegraff, Clarence M., *Arbitration and Labor Relations* (3rd ed.), BNA Books, 1970
A complete reference manual on the procedural, substantive, and practical aspects of labor arbitration.

Walton, Richard E., and Robert B. McKersie, *A Behavioral Theory of Labor Negotiations*. McGraw-Hill, 1965.
An original behavioral science analysis of the collective bargaining process.

Chapter 4—Personnel Planning

Fine, Sidney A., and Wretha W. Wiley, *An Introduction to Functional Job Analysis: A Scaling of Selected Tasks from the Social Welfare Field*. Upjohn Institute for Employment Research (Kalamazoo, Mich.), 1971.
Description of a procedure for establishing career ladders.

Ford, Robert N., *Motivation Through the Work Itself*. American Management Association, 1969.
Report of experiments with job enrichment programs in the Bell System.

Glueck, William F., *Organization Planning and Development*, American Management Association, 1971.
A study of the organizational planning and development function in a group of American companies.

Humble, John W. (ed.), *Management by Objectives in Action*. McGraw-Hill, 1970.
Series of articles outlining MBO concepts, practice, and programs.

Morrison, Edward J., *Developing Computer-Based Employee Information Systems*, American Management Association, 1969.
Review of the design and characteristics of existing employee information systems.

Prien, Erich P., and William W. Ronan, "Job Analysis: A Review of Research Findings," *Personnel Psychology*, Autumn 1971.
Comprehensive review of the research literature relating to job analysis.

Towers, Perrin, Forster, and Crosby (TPF/C), *Corporate Manpower Planning*. TPF/C (Philadelphia), 1971.
Survey of manpower planning activities in a group of large corporations.

Wikstrom, Walter S., *Manpower Planning: Evolving Systems*, The Conference Board, 1971.
Discussion of increased interest in manpower planning.

Chapter 5—Filling Jobs and Evaluating Job Performance

Byham, William C., "Assessment Centers for Spotting Future Managers," *Harvard Business Review*, July-August 1970.
Detailed description of the assessment center technique.

Carlson, Robert E., and others, "Improvements in the Selection Interview," *Personnel Journal*, April 1971.
Description of the results of a research program conducted by the Life Insurance Agency Management Association.

Dunnette, Marvin D., *Personnel Selection and Placement*, Wadsworth, 1966.
An outline of the logic of selection with strategies for personnel decisions.

Ghiselli, Edwin E., *The Validity of Occupational Aptitude Tests*, Wiley, 1969.
Comprehensive summary of research related to the effectiveness of various psychological tests.

Hawk, Roger H., *The Recruitment Function*, American Management Association, 1967.
Description of recruiting activities in industry.

Mandell, Milton, *The Selection Process*, American Management Association, 1964.
Discussion of selection techniques most useful for different groups and levels of employees.

Miner, John B., "Management Appraisal: A Capsule Review and Current References," *Business Horizons*, October 1968.
Evaluation of appraisal techniques and suggestions for effective programs.

Koontz, Harold, *Appraising Managers as Managers*, McGraw-Hill, 1971.
Description of a program emphasizing both appraisal against objectives and appraisal of managers as managers.

Lopez, Felix, *Personnel Interviewing: Theory and Practice*, McGraw-Hill, 1965.
Explanation of how interviewing relates to other personnel techniques.

Oberg, Winston, "Make Performance Appraisal Relevant," *Harvard Business Review*, January-February 1972.
Discussion of nine appraisal techniques indicating which ones are most effective for achieving different goals.

Chapter 6—Training and Development

Argyris, Chris, *Management and Organizational Development*, McGraw-Hill, 1971.
Presentation of a theory of organizational development and the results of experiments in three organizations.

Bass, Bernard M., and James A. Vaughn, *Training in Industry: The Management of Learning*, Wadsworth, 1966.
A review of learning theory as applied in the industrial setting.

Blake, Robert R., and Jane S. Mouton, *Corporate Excellence Through Grid Organization Development*, Gulf Publishing Co., 1968.
Description of the managerial grid approach to organization development.

Campbell, John D., and others, *Managerial Behavior, Performance, and Effectiveness*, McGraw-Hill, 1970.
A comparison of management development practices in government and industry with results of behavioral science research.

Craig, Robert L., and Lester R. Bittel (eds.), *Training and Development Handbook*, McGraw-Hill, 1967.
A comprehensive reference book covering all aspects of training and development.

Herzberg, Frederick W., *Work and the Nature of Man*, World, 1966.
An explanation and expansion of the two-factor theory of work motivation.

Janger, Allen R., and Ruth G. Shaeffer, *Managing Programs to Employ the Disadvantaged*, National Industrial Conference Board, 1970.
A summary analysis of programs for employing the disadvantaged in 100 companies with a detailed analysis of seven of the programs.

Likert, Rensis, *New Patterns of Management*, McGraw-Hill, 1961.
A report of research on groups in organizations with an explanation of the linking-pin concept.
——————————, *The Human Organization*, McGraw-Hill, 1967.
A philosophical statement of the System 4 concept of managerial styles.

Maslow, Abraham, *Eupsychian Management*, Irwin, 1965.
Description of a society inhabited by self-actualizing individuals.

McClelland, David C., and D. G. Winter, *Motivating Economic Achievement*, Free Press, 1969.
Report of results of efforts to raise the level of achievement motivation in a developing economy.

McGregor, Douglas, *The Human Side of Enterprise*, McGraw-Hill, 1960.
Presentation of the Theory X and Theory Y management approaches.

Miner, John B., *Studies in Management Education*, Springer, 1965.
Discussion of experimental designs for evaluating management training programs and presentation of a theory of managerial motivation with supporting research.

Rush, Harold M. F., *Behavioral Science: Concepts and Management Application*, National Industrial Conference Board, 1969.
An examination of behavioral science concepts from theory and research to application in organizations.

West, J. P., and D. R. Sheriff, *Executive Development Programs in Universities*, National Industrial Conference Board, 1969.
Outline of programs for executives offered by universities.

Chapter 7—Compensation

Allen, Donna, *Fringe Benefits: Wages or Social Obligations?*, Cornell University, 1969.
> An historical analysis indicating significant changes in status of fringe benefits.

Belcher, D. W., *Wage & Salary Administration*, Prentice-Hall, 1962.
> A standard text in the field.

Biegel, Herman C. and others, *Pensions and Profit-Sharing* (3rd ed.), BNA Books, 1964.
> Handbook of advice and guidance on various aspects of pension and profit-sharing plans.

Chamber of Commerce of the United States, *Employee Benefits, 1971*, The Chamber (Washington, D.C.), 1972.
> Most recent report on fringe benefit costs, issued biennially since 1947.

Crystal, Graef S., *Financial Motivation for Executives*, American Management Association, 1970.
> Presentation of a philosophy of executive compensation based on behavioral science theories.

Dunn, J. D. and Frank M. Rachel, *Wage and Salary Administration: Total Compensation Systems*, McGraw-Hill, 1971.
> Discussion of a systems approach to administration of a compensation program with illustrative cases.

Jaques, Elliot, *Equitable Payment: A General Theory of Work Differential Payment and Individual Progress*, Wiley, 1961.
> Basic prsentation of Jaques' equity theory.

Lawler, Edward E., *Pay and Organizational Effectiveness: A Psychological View*, McGraw-Hill, 1971.
> A treatment of pay policies as they affect human behavior and organizational effectiveness.

Livernash, E. Robert, "Wages and Benefits," in *A Review of Industrial Relations Research*, Vol. 1, Industrial Relations Research Association (Madison, Wis.), 1970.
> Review of research on wage administration and fringe benefits during the 1960's.

Nielsen, Niels H., "Running Benefits Like a Business," *Conference Board Record*, August 1970.
> Discussion advocating the consolidation of benefits management into a profit center.

Patton, J. A. and others, *Job Evaluation*, Irwin, 1964.
A textbook with case material.

Vroom, Victor H., *Work and Motivation*, New York, Wiley, 1964.
Exploration of aspects of motivation, including pay.

Chapter 8—Employee Relations and Communications

Alper, S. William and Stuart M. Klein, "Feedback Following Opinion Surveys," *Personnel Administration*, November-December 1970.
Report of a study of the feedback process and its effect on employee satisfaction.

Bassett, Glenn A., *The New Face of Communication*, American Management Association, 1968.
Discussion of ways to overcome communication barriers between superiors and subordinates.

Black, James M., *Positive Discipline*, American Management Association, 1970.
Exploration of all aspects of employee discipline emphasizing cooperative effort by manager and subordinates.

Davis, Keith, "Readability Changes in Employee Handbooks of Identical Companies During a Fifteen-Year Period," *Personnel Psychology*, Winter 1968.
Comparison of 29 company handbooks from 1949 to 1964.

Dickson, William J. and F. J. Roethlisberger, *Counseling in an Organization: A Sequel to the Hawthorne Researches*, Harvard University Graduate School of Business Administration, 1966.
An analysis of the counseling experience with production workers that was an outgrowth of the Hawthorne studies.

Dover, C. J., *Management Communication on Controversial Issues*, BNA Books, 1965.
A critique of management communication on such issues as strikes and other aspects of union relations and company financial affairs.

Foulkes, Fred K., *Creating More Meaningful Work*, American Management Association, 1969.
Examination of a variety of approaches to increase the meaningfulness of work at the nonmanagement level.

Gilmore, Charles L., *Accident Prevention and Loss Control*, American Management Association, 1970.
Proposal for an efficient program for controlling real or potential loss from accidents.

Haddon, William, Edward A. Suchman, and David Klein, *Accident Research: Methods and Approaches*, Harper & Row, 1964.
Discussion of significant studies in accident research and the methodology of the studies.

Habbe, Stephen, *Company Controls for Drinking Problems*, National Industrial Conference Board, 1968.
Survey of the problems, company practices and programs, and resources available for handling the alcoholic employee.

Kornhauser, Arthur, *Mental Health of the Industrial Worker: A Detroit Study*, Wiley, 1965.
Discussion of the influence of the work environment on employee mental health and behavior.

Miner, John B., *Introduction to Industrial Clinical Psychology*, McGraw-Hill, 1966.
Discussion of why people fail on the job and techniques for coping with ineffective performance.

Myers, M. Scott, *Every Employee a Manager: More Meaningful Work Through Job Enrichment*, McGraw-Hill, 1970.
Explanation of job enrichment with examples of company programs and techniques.

Petersen, Daniel C., *Techniques of Safety Management*, McGraw-Hill, 1971.
An outline of areas of the safety profession that are increasingly important in industry.

Rush, Harold M. F., *Job Design for Motivation: Experiments in Job Enlargement and Job Enrichment*, Conference Board, 1971.
Discussion of the historical and theoretical influences on the job design movement and the predominant methods used.

Stessin, Lawrence, *Employee Discipline*, BNA Books, 1960.
Explanation of how to apply discipline and protect the rights of both management and the employee.

Summers, Gene F. (ed.), *Attitude Measurement*, Rand McNally, 1970.
A book of articles and other writings on attitude measurement techniques.

Trotta, Maurice S., *Insubordination*, BNA Incorporated, 1967.
Presentation of cases to help distinguish between apparent and real insubordination.

TOPICAL INDEX

A

B

C